SPIRAL GUIDES

Travel With Someone You Trust®

W9-BOM-277

WASHINGTON D.C.

Contents

the magazine 5

Finding Your Feet 33

The East Mall 45

The West Mall 75

Written by Paul Franklin
"Where to…" sections by Shane Christensen and Margaret Foster

Updated by Paul Franklin

American editor Tracy Larson

Edited, designed and produced by AA Publishing
© Automobile Association Developments Limited 2006, 2008
Maps © Automobile Association Developments Limited 2006, 2008

Published in the United States by AAA Publishing,
1000 AAA Drive, Heathrow, Florida 32746-5063
Published in the United Kingdom by AA Publishing

ISBN-13: 978-1-59508-248-0

Cover design and binding style by permission of AA Publishing
Color separation by Keenes, Andover
Printed and bound in China by Leo Paper Products

10 9 8 7 6 5 4 3 2 1

A03183

the magazine

Powertown,

In the 2000 movie *Thirteen Days*, President John F. Kennedy's political adviser, Kenny O'Donnell (played by Kevin Costner), crosses names off a list of party guests drawn up by Jacqueline Kennedy. "Who are all these people?" asks O'Donnell. "They're friends," replies Jacqueline. "Yeah, but they're not votes," retorts O'Donnell. Many Washington insiders would say that that interaction pretty well sums up Washington's primary subculture. If Los Angeles is the city of fame and New York the city of money, then Washington is the city of political power *par excellence*.

Washington's very existence is a result of political wranglings. Long before the Civil War, there were tensions between the Northern and Southern states and early attempts to locate the seat of government in Boston or Philadelphia were met with strong resistance from the Southerners.

As part of a compromise in 1790, it was decided that a new capital city would be built in the country, not in an existing state (which might get special benefits as a

U.S.A.

result), but in a specially designated district.

Ironically for a city that exists for political power, Washington's citizens have very little say in their own affairs.

Until 1964, they could not vote in a Federal election and they have had little control over the city's operation, which is governed by Congress. In 1970, they got their first (non-voting) seat in the House of Representatives. In 1973, The Home Rule Charter was ratified, and for the first time in a century they elected a mayor. But the district remains under Congressional jurisdiction, and the people still do not have voting Federal representatives, making them the least politically powerful citizens of the most politically powerful city in the world.

The American Political System

America's political system has three primary branches of government: The executive, the legislative and the judicial. These three branches have a unique, interdependent relationship: Each requires the cooperation of the others to make changes, and each has the ability to nullify the decisions of the other. This system of "checks and balances" is often praised as the cornerstone on which the nation's stability rests. It also is cursed for resulting in a slow-moving government and watered-down decision-making.

The White House and Senate offices are where bills are amended and deals are often made

Opposite:
The Willard Intercontinental Washington is a popular meeting place for lobbyists and politicians

Houses of Power: Where the Decisions Are Made

The White House (▶110–114)

The policies and decisions of the executive branch are made here. The president is commander-in-chief of all military forces, and is responsible for setting foreign policy, negotiating treaties, and implementing domestic policies that are designed to enhance the country's financial and social well-being.

The president is assisted by his cabinet, which includes the secretaries of state, defense, interior, education and others.

The Capitol Building (▶138–141)

The Capitol is home to the legislative branch of government – Congress – which comprises the House of Representatives (the lower house) and the Senate (the upper house).

It is their responsibility to create the country's laws. A new law starts as a bill, introduced in either the House or the Senate. The House of Representatives can change or amend a bill, and if it passes a vote, it moves on to the Senate, which also can amend the bill and pass it, or return it to the House for more work. If the bill passes, it then goes to the president, who can either sign it into law or veto it. If the president vetoes a bill, it returns to Congress, where a two-thirds majority vote in each house can override the president's veto and pass it into law.

Senators and Representatives are elected by the public, and neither are required to vote along party lines. There are 435 seats in the House of Representatives, which are divided among the states according to population. Each state also elects two senators, giving every state an equal voice in the Senate.

The Supreme Court (▶ 152)

The nine Supreme Court justices hear cases here and represent the highest level of the judicial branch of government. It has been said that the Supreme Court is the most powerful arm of the government, for it alone has the final say on what is or is not legal and constitutional.

Other Houses of Power

Willard InterContinental Washington (▶ 41)

Washington's army of lobbyists represents interests as diverse as manufacturing, pro- and anti-gun groups, environmental causes and civil rights groups. Although today they practice their trade in offices and public places throughout the city, the hotel is often considered their spiritual home. Since the 1800s, the luxurious lobby of the Willard has been one of their favorite places to meet and try to influence

political decisions. It was here that the term "lobbyist" was coined.

The Pentagon

The Pentagon, which controls a budget of $400 billion, is headquarters of the Department of Defense. Top personnel from all branches of the armed forces advise the president on state matters and military defense.

The Oval Office is perhaps the most famous workspace in the world

Extremely close presidential elections

John Quincy Adams was considered a brilliant orator but an ineffective president

Thomas Jefferson vs. Aaron Burr

In 1800, Jefferson and Burr each received 73 electoral votes, which meant Congress had to determine the outcome. Some last-minute making of deals by Jefferson gave him the congressional vote on the 36th ballot, but only on the condition that he take Burr, whom he deeply mistrusted, as his vice president. Jefferson acquiesced, but later Burr was completely shut out of the decision-making process.

John Quincy Adams vs. Andrew Jackson

In 1824, there were four candidates, and although Andrew Jackson won the greatest number of both popular and electoral votes,

he did not win the required majority, so again, it was up to Congress to choose the president. Powerful lobbying by Henry Clay swayed the House in Adams's favor. But the voters had their revenge four years later when they elected Jackson president in a landslide victory.

John F. Kennedy vs. Richard Nixon

In 1960, John F. Kennedy won by a substantial margin in the Electoral College, but by an extremely narrow margin of the popular vote. Kennedy, however, helped unify the parties by selecting several Republicans for his cabinet and taking a middle-of-the-road stance on domestic and foreign affairs.

George and Al Go To College

Although the Bush-Kerry presidential contest of 2004 was not close enough to raise eyebrows, the 2000 election brought to the world's attention one of the most confusing aspects of the American electoral process, the Electoral College system.

Created as a part of the Constitution, the Electoral College was designed to balance the voting power of larger and smaller states. In the electoral system, each state's number of electoral votes is based on the total number of its congressmen and senators (Florida, for instance, has 25 seats in the House and two senators, therefore 27 electoral votes).

In every state, except Maine and Nebraska, the winner of the popular vote wins all of a state's electors, not a proportion of them. That is how, in very close elections, a candidate with a small lead in the popular vote can still lose the electoral vote.

Best Washington Power Bars

The oldest and most famous bar for possibly spotting a politico is the **Hawk 'n' Dove** (329 Pennsylvania Avenue, tel: 202/543-3300, ➤ 158), frequented by politicians and lobbyists alike.

You also might glimpse movers and shakers at the **Capitol Lounge** (229 Pennsylvania Avenue, tel: 202/547-2098), an upscale Capitol Hill cigar and martini bar.

Best Beer

If you don't care about seeing bigwigs but just want a cold brew to quench your thirst, try the **Brickskeller** (1523 22nd Street N.W., ➤ 103), which serves more than 1,000 varieties of beer and whose bartenders all have a Ph.D. in Beer-ology.

The cheapest beer in town ($2/pint, including imports) is at **Common Share** (2003 18th Street N.W., tel: 202/518-6881).

One of Georgetown's finest homes, Dumbarton Oaks and its gardens are open to the public

Washington Bests and Mosts

The Tourmobile is a fun and economical way to see Washington's best sights

Bird-watchers along the Potomac

a knockout, encompassing the Mall, Smithsonian museums, monuments and the Potomac.

Best Gardens

The most elaborate public gardens are at **Hillwood Museum** (▶ 124). Visits require advance reservations.

Slightly smaller, but just as beautiful and more easily accessible, are the 10 acres (4ha) of gardens surrounding the elegant **Dumbarton Oaks** mansion (▶ 123).

Washington's best-hidden oasis is **Bishop's Garden**, a sanctuary at the Washington National Cathedral (▶ 124).

Best Views of the City

The best classic view of Washington is from the steps of the **Lincoln Memorial** (▶ 86–87), which takes in the entire length of the Mall, the World War II Memorial, the Washington Monument and the Capitol Building. You can see essentially the same view, but with more of Washington, from the porch of Arlington House in **Arlington National Cemetery** (▶ 89–92).

The view from the West Portico of the **Capitol Building** (▶ 138–141) is also

Best Tours

The **Tourmobile** (▶ 89–90) is a National Park Service concession that stops at all the major attractions between Capitol Hill and Arlington National Cemetery. You pay

one daily ticket price and can get on and off as many times as you like. It runs every 30 minutes daily 9:30–4:30 (expensive, tel: 202/554-7950).

Best Bird-Watching

Two consistently favored destinations for bird-watching are **Theodore Roosevelt Island** (➤ 98) and **Hains Point**, at the tip of East Potomac Park (➤ 99). Both offer a good blend of land and water habitats that have a variety of species year-round.

Best Washington Adventures

Of course, most of the high adventure in Washington takes place in the political arena. But for more low-key thrills, your best bet is a **bicycle trip along the C&O Canal** (➤ 122–123), or

paddling a kayak or canoe down the Potomac River.

You can rent both bicycles for the canal towpath and kayaks or canoes for river adventures at **Thompson's Boat Center** in Georgetown (2900 Virginia Avenue N.W., tel: 202/333-4861).

If You Go To Only One...

...**memorial**, make it the Lincoln Memorial (➤ 86–88).

...**gallery**, make it the National Gallery of Art (➤ 54–58).

...**museum**, make it the National Air and Space Museum (➤ 50–53).

...**government building**, make it the White House (➤ 110–114).

...**park**, make it the C&O Canal National Historic Park (➤ 122–123).

The bright red northern cardinal is a frequent visitor to Washington gardens

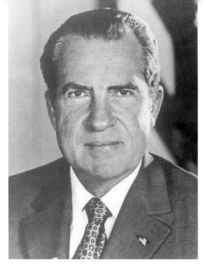

The Mother of All Scandals

Like a good Shakespearian play, Watergate offered a *potpourri* of high tragedy and low comedy, with some of the most memorable political moments of the 20th century. Stone-faced President Richard Nixon declaring to the world, "I am not a crook!" cannot easily be forgotten.

This particular scandal began in the early hours of June 17, 1972, when Washington police arrested five "well-dressed" burglars at the headquarters of the National Democratic Committee in the

The Scanda

Washingtonians love a good scandal. From the earliest days, when members of Congress accused George Washington of padding his expense account, this city and its scandals have been inextricably linked, with the most unforgettable revolving around political power.

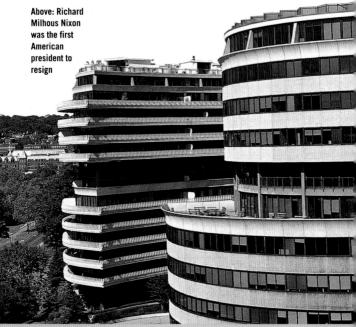

Above: Richard Milhous Nixon was the first American president to resign

Watergate complex. Among those arrested was Frank McCord, an ex-CIA operative, who was a security adviser to the Republican Committee to Re-elect the President.

Although it has never been proved, the popular theory is that the burglars, working for Republican interests, were attempting to bug the office of NDC Chairman Lawrence O'Brian to obtain Democratic election strategy information.

Police eventually determined that the burglars had been under the direction of former White House aides E. Howard Hunt and G. Gordon Liddy, but they were unable to take the investigation further.

The Republicans vigorously denied any knowledge of the

Ex-CIA employee James McCord

Factory

What's In a Name?
Forever linked with scandal, Watergate is a modern complex of offices, condominiums, restaurants, shops and a first-class hotel, near the John F. Kennedy Center on the banks of the Potomac. It was originally named for the broad sweep of ceremonial steps rising from the riverbank, where visiting dignitaries used to arrive by boat (ergo, Water Gate).

burglary, and the whole incident may have been forgotten had it not been for the dogged determination of two young *Washington Post* reporters, Bob Woodward and Carl Bernstein, who believed that there was a much bigger story to be uncovered. They were aided by the *Post*'s executive editor, Ben Bradlee, and by Woodward's mysterious, politically connected informant known only as "Deep Throat," who urged them to "follow the money."

grew the FBI stepped up its investigation and the Senate also got involved, convening the Watergate Hearings.

While many experts believe that Nixon knew of the burglary from the beginning, this has never been proved.

What toppled the president was his active participation in the cover-up, trying to get the CIA to impede the FBI's investigation, discussing cover-up strategies with Special White House Council John Dean and also having

Woodward and Bernstein broke the story that one of the burglars had been paid by a check earmarked for the Committee to Re-Elect the President (CRP, ironically known as "creep").

They also discovered that a huge CRP slush fund, used to finance a widespread campaign of dirty tricks against the Democrats, was controlled by top Nixon aides including John Ehrlichman, J. R. Haldeman and ex-Attorney General John Mitchell.

These revelations stunned the nation. As public furor

Watergate Special Prosecutor Archibald Cox fired.

In July 1974, the Supreme Court ordered Nixon to turn over 64 key "White House tapes" that he himself had made of his conversations. He did, but held back three tapes, angering friends and foes alike.

On August 5, under enormous pressure, Nixon released the final three tapes, which clearly established his active role in the cover-up following the Watergate break-in.

Four days later, on August 9, 1974, he became the first American president to resign office. Vice President Gerald

Ford took over the presidency and eventually issued Nixon a full presidential pardon. The Watergate scandal changed Washington's political landscape, tainting the city's aura as a bastion of democracy.

But it also began a process of sweeping campaign finance reforms and created the expectation, if not the reality, of greater accountability at every level of government.

Deep Throat Revealed

For three decades one of the most popular pastimes on the Washington cocktail circuit was trying to guess the identity of the mysterious but politically powerful informant who helped Woodard in his investigations. In May 2005, Mark Felt, who was the number two man at the FBI during Watergate, announced that he had been "Deep Throat." So what made a hardened "G man" an informant? Felt has said that he was motivated by frustration after the Nixon administration placed L. Patrick Gray in charge of the FBI. Felt feared that Gray would allow the White House to direct or even stall the investigation.

Scandals Great and Small

Thomas and Sally

Thomas Jefferson's presidency was plagued by rumors that his fondness for his slaves had reached an all-time high when he had a long affair (and several children) with one of his house slaves, Sally Hemings. Denied by Jefferson supporters for more than 200 years, it was finally proved by DNA testing.

CIA Means Never Having To Say You're Sorry

The 1986 Iran-Contra scandal had everything: clandestine meetings, a noble hero, a beautiful woman, international arms deals and lots of skullduggery. The story was that the CIA, forbidden by Congress to support the rebels in Nicaragua, secretly sold arms to Iran and gave the money to the Contras.

Key players were Oliver North, who shredded incriminating documents, his blond assistant Fawn Hall, and President Ronald Reagan, who claimed to have napped through the whole thing.

John Dean, Special White House Council, testifying during the Watergate scandal

Colonel Oliver North was a key figure in the Iran-Contra affair

Washingtonians love to tell newcomers how awful their traffic is. In fact, complaining about Capital gridlock and its associated horrors, fender-benders and road rage can seem to outsiders to be the No. 1 topic of polite conversation after politics. This is not without good reason, however, as all too often you simply can't get there from here. Twice each day, the city's already busy streets congeal as tens of thousands of workers try to enter or exit the city on avenues designed 200 years ago for horse-and-carriage traffic. And at any time of day, the notorious Capital Beltway can instantly become the world's longest parking lot. In fact, a recent study stated what Washingtonians have long known: They spend more time stuck in traffic than anyone else in the nation.

Capital Gridlock

So why, in this bastion of forward-thinking leadership, do so many spend so much time going nowhere?

Part of the problem has been the dynamic growth and shift of the population. Since the 1950s, while the city population has shrunk slightly to about 550,000, the suburban population has tripled to more than 5 million, many of whom commute daily into the city.

In the 1950s, a comprehensive program of highway development was begun that involved building 369 miles (594km) of superhighways.

According to a recent study, Washingtonians spend more time in traffic jams than anyone else in the U.S.

The plan included an eight-lane bridge across the Potomac River, highways to the major suburbs, and five concentric circles of freeways around the city. Several factors contributed to the demise of this plan. Environmentalists felt that additional bridges across the Potomac River would harm valuable wildlife habitat. Civil rights activists pointed out that the city neighborhoods that would be leveled for new highways were predominantly black and poor. And historical preservationists got into the act, citing the number of important buildings that would have to be destroyed to make room for the highways. In the end, the only highway built was the Capital Beltway, plus a few stretches of freeway that often bewilder visitors by seeming to start and stop in the middle of nowhere.

However, there is an excellent alternative to driving around D.C. The city's gleaming Metro subway system was completed at a cost of $10 billion, making it the most expensive public works project in U.S. history. The system is clean and safe and offers fast, comfortable transit to almost anywhere in the downtown area. The system also serves suburbs in Virginia and Maryland.

Unlike the efficient subway system, Metro's bus system is archaic and slow. But private bus services such as Supershuttle offer fast access to the outlying airports.

Background: Traffic on the Capital Beltway often comes to a standstill

Washington's ultramodern Metro subway system gets you from here to there quickly and in style

GREAT GATHERINGS

On a steamy August day in 1963, a large man walked up the steps of the Lincoln Memorial (▶ 86–88) and took his place before a microphone. Before him lay a sea of faces: 250,000 people, mostly African-Americans, had walked to the capital from places like Alabama, Georgia and Mississippi, as well as cities in the North. It was the largest gathering of people in the nation's history. As he began to speak, his rich orator's voice rose and fell with words that captivated not just his audience but, via television and radio, an entire nation:

"I have a dream that one day this nation will rise up and live out the true meaning of its creed: 'We hold these truths to be self-evident: that *all* men are created equal.' I have a dream that one day on the red hills of Georgia, the sons of former slaves and the sons of former slave owners will be able to sit down together at the table of brotherhood...I have a dream that my four little children will one day live in a nation where they will not be judged by the color of their skin but by the content of their character. ..."

The man, of course, was Martin Luther King, Jr., whose "I Have a Dream" speech became a touchstone for the civil rights movement, and is

Background:
The Bonus March in 1932 protested against how veterans from the armed forces had been treated

considered one of the greatest American speeches of all time.

It was no accident that King chose the steps of the Lincoln Memorial from which to make his speech. Lincoln, the Great Emancipator, is a symbol of freedom to African-Americans. But more than that, the National Mall itself, that great lawn in the heart of the nation's capital, has been a favorite gathering place for groups promoting their causes since the early 1900s.

The Lincoln Memorial was the site of one of the first civil rights protests, albeit a gentle and musical one, in 1939. The popular contralto opera singer Marian Anderson was denied permission to sing at Constitution Hall by the Daughters of the American Revolution (DAR) because she was African-American. When first lady Eleanor Roosevelt, a member of the DAR herself, learned of the situation, she was outraged. In a highly publicized action, she resigned from the DAR and helped Ms. Anderson to arrange a free concert from the steps of the Lincoln Memorial. Over 75,000 people turned out to hear the singer, who opened her concert with the song "America," whose lyrics begin: "My country 'tis of thee, sweet land of liberty, of thee I sing."

Not every gathering on the Mall has had such high ideals. One of the first large

Martin Luther King, Jr. salutes the people who came from all over America to hear him speak

gatherings occurred in 1925, when more than 25,000 Ku Klux Klan members assembled here. This notorious group espoused white supremacy and the absolute separation of the races. They protested what they saw as a growing trend toward racial integration and civil rights. Although they usually dressed in long white robes with pointed hoods that concealed their identities, for this event they marched with their hoods rolled up, claiming they had nothing to feel ashamed of.

From this less than auspicious start, an impressive number of protests, marches and rallies has taken place on the National Mall. The following highlights some larger marches, rallies and protests that have taken place over the past 75 years.

1932: The Bonus March

At the height of the Great Depression, more than 20,000 veterans and their families made their way to Washington to protest their desperate condition. Most of them were penniless, without education or the means to improve their lives, which they saw as poor payment for their service in the armed services. Specifically, they were protesting the government's decision to put off the promised payment of a $1,000 service bonus. Many lived for months in shantytowns in Washington, but eventually their action forced the government's creation of the GI Bill of Rights, which gives veterans assistance with housing and education, better employment opportunities and free medical care.

1968: The Poor People's March

This protest was originally planned by Martin Luther King, Jr., who tragically was

assassinated just a few months before it began. Three thousand poor people marched from across the United States, converging on Washington and setting up and living in a shantytown by the Lincoln Memorial. Without King's leadership the protest lacked direction and few immediate benefits were achieved.

1987: The Names Project

At its debut, the AIDS Quilt was unrolled on the National Mall. Covering a space the size of a football field, the quilt contained more than 1,900 hand-sewn panels, each with the name of a person who had died from AIDS. That weekend more than half a million people came to see the quilt. When it was unrolled in 1996, it had over 38,000 panels.

1995: The Million Man March

Organized by controversial Nation of Islam leader Louis Farrakhan, as many as 500,000 mostly African-American men participated in this huge rally on the Mall, during which they pledged to "clean up their lives and rebuild their neighborhoods."

2000: The Million Mom March

Comedian Rosie O'Donnell and first lady Hillary Clinton led several hundred thousand mothers, who gathered on the National Mall to demand tougher gun laws.

2004: The March for Women's Lives

Organizers say that over 1 million people participated in this march for women's reproductive rights, making it the largest in the city's history.

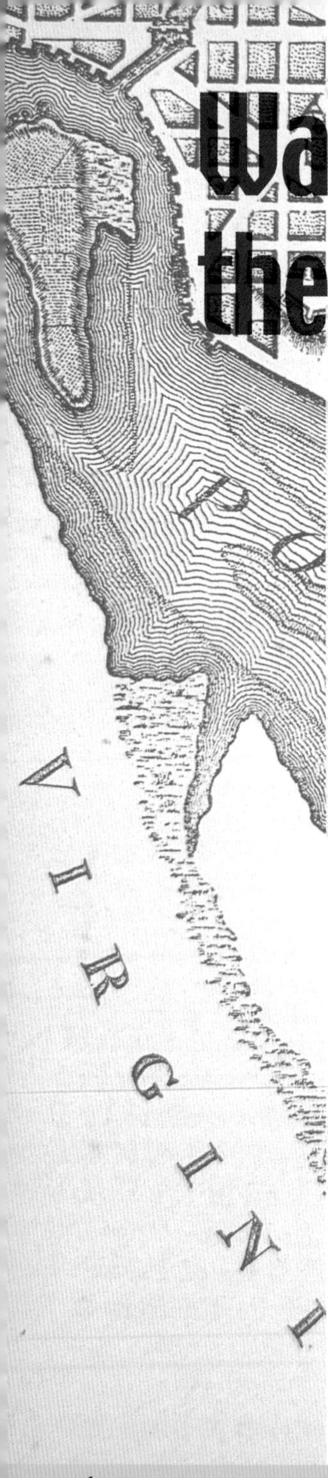

Water Under the Bridge:

Pages from Washington's Past

He'll Never Eat Lunch in This Town Again...

The first federal employee to be fired in Washington was city designer Pierre L'Enfant, in 1792. A French artist and soldier, L'Enfant had served with George Washington during the Revolution. He was a visionary, but could also be hardheaded and abrasively aristocratic, and he infuriated landowners when they realized that he had used more than half of the available land (which they intended to sell profitably as city lots) for grand boulevards. He also refused to publicly display his plan, without which no one was willing to purchase building lots, leaving both the landowners and government short of money.

The final straw came when a nephew of one of the city commissioners began building a new manor house that disrupted one of L'Enfant's view lines. While the owner was away, L'Enfant had the structure torn down. George Washington had no choice but to fire him, although the government continued to use his plan. He was offered

Background: Pierre L'Enfant's grand plan for Washington was both ambitious and visionary, and much of his design was eventually built

$2,500 and a prime city lot for his efforts. He refused, but later tried unsuccessfully to sue. He eventually died a poor and broken man.

The Man Who Would Be King

In 1804, Vice President Aaron Burr (one of the founders of Chase Manhattan Bank) challenged his long-term political enemy, Alexander Hamilton, to a duel, and killed him. Burr returned to Washington and coolly resumed his duties as vice president while New York and New Jersey considered pressing charges for murder (eventually all were dropped).

and take control of the vast Louisiana Purchase, creating his own country. Eventually one of his co-conspirators, General James Wilkinson, betrayed him to President Thomas Jefferson, who ordered Burr be arrested for treason. Burr turned himself in to the local authorities, but later escaped and was recaptured. He was acquitted on a technicality and spent most of the rest of his life in Europe.

Hot Time In The New Town

During the War of 1812, British forces under Admiral George Cockburn attacked Washington. President James Madison left the White House

After shooting and killing Alexander Hamilton in a duel, Aaron Burr returned to Washington to resume the duties of vice president

When his term as vice president ended, he headed for the Western frontier, obtained more than a million acres of land, and began to gather armed men and supplies.

Accounts differ as to his intentions, but it was believed he planned to conquer Mexico

to supervise the defense of the city, while his wife Dolley remained behind until the last moment. Hastily loading a wagon with valuables, she refused to leave until the now famous Gilbert Stuart portrait of George Washington had been placed in safekeeping.

Shortly after she left, the British arrived at the White House and were surprised to find a feast for 40, optimistically prepared to celebrate an American victory. Not ones to waste an opportunity, they sat down to a good meal before torching the house.

The Legend of "Boss" Shepherd

Perhaps no man has been more praised or cursed for making L'Enfant's grand plan for Wash-

injunctions could be written. After tripling the city's debt by spending more than $20 million in two years, he was fired. Congress, however, had no choice but to finish all the projects he had started, finally creating the city that L'Enfant had envisioned.

A Roma Americae

During the building of the Washington Monument, many states and foreign governments donated memorial

ington a reality than Alexander Roby "Boss" Shepherd.

In 1870, Washington was still a town of dirt streets and shanty homes. A wealthy businessman, Shepherd used his charismatic leadership to rise to the top of the public works department. With little grasp of engineering, he launched scores of building projects, leaving a town of half-finished streets, sewers, parks and schools. He was also not above lining his own pockets. In one case, he built a new market (which he invested in), then had a competing market torn down while entertaining the town justices at his home one night so that no last-minute

stones to its construction. One of these, inscribed *A Roma Americae* (From Rome to America) was from the Pope. But in 1854 members of the passionately nationalist and anti-Catholic American Party (unofficially called the "Know-Nothings" because whenever something illegal took place they claimed to "know nothing") stole the stone at gunpoint, then broke it into small pieces and threw it into the Potomac River. The Know-Nothings had convinced themselves that the Pope had a secret plan to relocate the Holy See in America. The perpetrators were never caught, and it was

In 1814, the British Army marched into Washington and burned many prominent buildings, including the White House and Capitol Building

well over a century before the stone was replaced, in 1982.

The Empress of Washington

A senator's wife and society diva, Mrs. John B. Henderson had a lifelong dream of living in a magnificent house in a magnificent neighborhood. In the late 1880s, she began to impose her dream on Washington. She started by buying up large lots of land along an undeveloped portion of 16th Street. After having a castlelike house built for herself, she added mansions and villas which she sold to wealthy friends (for a healthy profit). Her goal was to see the White House relocated to her neighborhood. The closest she came, however, was to get 16th Street renamed "The Avenue of the Presidents," a change that only lasted two years before neighbors, who felt the name was too ostentatious, changed it back.

At the start of the Civil War, construction was halted on the Washington Monument, and for years it remained unfinished

Ask about Washington's performing arts scene and you're likely to hear the common refrain: "Well, it's not New York." But Washington offers more performing arts events per capita than either New York or Los Angeles.

This is a city fairly bursting at the seams with theater, opera, dance and every kind of music from baroque to steamy salsa and grit-kicking the **Performing Arts** (► 132). This gleaming, modernistic building overlooks the Potomac River and its 2,500-seat concert hall has world-class acoustics. The Kennedy Center is the official home of the National Symphony Orchestra, led by Leonard Slatkin, and guest soloists have included Joshua Bell, Kyung Wha Chung and Pinchas Zucharman.

THE BARD ON

country. Not surprisingly, this is exactly how our Founding Fathers envisioned that "The Rome of the New World" would turn out. (Well, maybe they didn't know about salsa.)

Historically, whenever there is a blend of wealth and political power, enjoyment of the arts at their very best is never far behind. Washington's budget comes from Congress, a group not known for their restraint when it comes to having a good time.

The flagship of the performing arts scene is the **John F. Kennedy Center for**

But the Kennedy Center is not just for orchestral music. Its facilities include a 2,200-seat opera house and four smaller theaters that host a variety of stage and musical productions. In all, the center presents more than 3,000 performances every year, including opera, theater, ballet, jazz and pop.

Washington's second internationally famous venue is **Wolf Trap Farm Park**. The only national park dedicated solely to the performing arts, it is just 15 minutes' drive from downtown Washington on a wooded reserve in northern Virginia.

Variety is the spice of Wolf Trap's life. Performers have included such diverse talents as Ladysmith Black Mombazo, the Tokyo String Quartet and the Austin

Below: The John F. Kennedy Center is one of the best venues for opera, symphony and theatrical performances

Bottom: See a show at Wolf Trap Farm Park

THE MALL

Lounge Lizards. The Farm's huge Eileen Center, with indoor and lawn seating, is where the major acts play. For some Washingtonians, an evening's outing to Wolf Trap with a picnic basket and blanket to spread on the grass has become a tradition.

For Shakespeare lovers, no city in America can compare to Washington. The best place to see the Bard's plays performed in an Elizabethan-style theater-in-the-round is at the **Folger Shakespeare Library** (► 151–152), near the Capitol.

The acclaimed performances at the **Shakespeare Theatre** (➤ 74) at 450 7th Street N.W. are frequently sold out months in advance.

The most fun way to experience the dramatic excellence of the Shakespeare Theatre is at a summertime performance at the beautiful, open-air **Carter Barron Amphitheater** in Rock Creek Park (➤ 123). The amphitheater also hosts a variety of events including jazz, soul and R&B.

Lincoln's time, and specializes in classic American plays such as *To Kill a Mockingbird*.

DAR (Daughters of the American Revolution) **Constitution Hall** (➤ 104), one of Washington's oldest auditoriums, presents a variety of acts from Whitney Houston to Wynton Marsalis and Burt Bacharach.

The small, funky **Woolly Mammoth Theatre** (➤ 132) specializes in cutting-edge plays and world premiers.

"The Rome of the New World"

Almost every American president has attended performances at the **National Theatre** (➤ 132) since it opened in 1835. The National is the oldest theater in the city, specializing in major Broadway productions.

Just around the corner, the richly decorated **Warner Theatre** (➤ 74) presents a selection of mainstream music acts and smaller-scale Broadway shows.

Nearby is the historic **Ford's Theatre** (➤ 69), where Abraham Lincoln was assassinated in 1865. The theater has been meticulously restored to look as it did in

Last, and perhaps best, is **Arena Stage** (➤ 74), a serious theatergoer's theater. Famous for its interpretations of such classics as *A Streetcar Named Desire*, it has won over 50 Helen Hayes Awards and the first Tony for Theatrical Excellence awarded outside New York.

If your idea of performing arts has more to do with exploring Washington's glittering nightlife, you're in luck again. The jazz bars, nightclubs and rock palaces of Dupont Circle,

EUROPE
1927

Georgetown and Adams-Morgan neighborhoods offer enough variety and excitement to keep anyone busy for weeks.

Rock 'n' Roll lovers should try **Rock and Roll Hotel** (1353 H Street N.E.) or big-name mainstream acts, **9:30 Club** (815 V Street N.W.) for alternative rock and pop, and **Black Cat** (1811 14th Street N.W.) foreverything else.

Jazz lovers should make a pilgrimage to the small **Blues Alley** (▶ 132), a renowned Georgetown jazz bar on Wisconsin Avenue

Or there's the **Bohemian Caverns**, whose legendary U Street stage has hosted such jazz greats as Louis Armstrong, Duke Ellington and John Coltrane.

And if you're a salsa fan you could sway the night away to the sexy beat at **Zanzibar on the Waterfront** on Water Street.

Tickets

The easiest way to get tickets for events is to call one of the ticket agencies below:

Tickets.com: 800/955-5566
Ticketmaster: 202/397-7328 or 800/551-7328
Ticket Place: 202/842-5387

Or you can call the venue direct:
Arena Stage: 202/488-3300
Black Cat: 202/667-7960
Blues Alley 202/337-4141
Bohemian Caverns: 202/299-0800
Carter Barron Amphitheater: 202/426-0486
DAR Constitution Hall: 202/628-4780
Ford's Theatre: 202/347-4833
Folger Shakespeare Library: 202/544-7077
John F. Kennedy Center for the Performing Arts: 202/467-4600
Rock and Roll Hotel: 202/388-7625
National Theatre: 202/628-6161
9:30 Club: 202/393-0930
Shakespeare Theatre: 202/547-1122
Warner Theatre: 202/783-4000
Washington Ballet: 202/362-3606
Washington National Opera: 202/295-2420 or 800/876-7372
Wolf Trap Farm Park: 703/255-1860
Woolly Mammoth Theatre: 202/393-3939
Zanzibar on the Waterfront: 202/554-9100

The Albert Einstein Planetarium

A state-of-the-art, digital Sky Vision system and Zeiss planetarium projector along with six-channel digital surround-sound serve up a 20-minute tour of the universe.

✚ 195E2 ✉ Independence Avenue at 4th Street S.W.
☎ 202/633-4629;
www.nasm.si.edu/visit/theaters/planetarium
🚇 Smithsonian

Ben's Chili Bowl

A great place for hot dogs, hamburgers, fries, shakes and chili in a landmark 1950s-style diner with bright red booths and thumping hip-hop music. Fun for everyone.

✚ 195 E2 ✉ 1213 U Street N.W. ☎ 202/667-0909
🚇 U Street/Cardozo

International Spy Museum

Kids can have a great time here. The museum examines both the real and fictional worlds of secret agents. Learn about how spies are trained and examine real spy gadgets including tiny cameras, bugs and even James Bond's car. Regular children's programs.

✚ 195 D4 ✉ 800 F Street
☎ 866/779-6873 or 202/393-7798; www.spymuseum.org
🚇 Chinatown

National Air and Space Museum (► 50–53)

Children will love the amazing displays, from the Wright Brothers' 1903 flyer to the *Viking Mars Lander*, and even a moon rock. Wright Place Food Court offers food for aspiring astronauts.

✚ 194 E2 ✉ Independence Avenue at 4th Street S.W. (between 6th and 7th Streets)
☎ 202/633-1000 🚇 L'Enfant Plaza, Smithsonian

National Museum of Natural History (► 59–61)

Mouths drop at the sight of the Dinosaur Hall, the Discovery Center, and the world's largest blue diamond.

✚ 1195 D3 ✉ 10th Street and Constitution Avenue N.W.
☎ 202/633-1000 🚇 Federal Triangle

National Zoological Park (► 119–220)

What child will not adore the pandas, be amazed as apes learn to use computers, be mesmerized by the sights and sounds of Amazonia? This is no ordinary zoo!

✚ 197 E5 ✉ 3001 Connecticut Avenue N.W.
☎ 202/633-4800 🚇 Woodley Park/Zoo, Cleveland Park

Items on display at the International Spy Museum

Finding Your Feet

First Two Hours

Washington, D.C. is served by three airports: Ronald Reagan Washington National Airport (DCA), Washington Dulles International Airport (IAD) and Baltimore-Washington International Airport (BWI). Each offers a variety of transportation alternatives into the city.

Ground Transportation Fees
(including tolls, if any, but excluding tip)
$ under $12 $$ $12–$20 $$$ $20–$30 $$$$ over $30

Best Bets for Airport to City Transportation

- **SuperShuttle,** a private van service, offers regular runs from all three airports to major points downtown. Single-passenger rates are slightly less than taxi rates. Services offer reduced rates for additional passengers.
- **Hotel shuttles** are provided by many hotels and are free to and from the airports. If you don't have a room reserved but know of a hotel near your destination, you may be able to ride in their shuttle for a modest fee.
- **Taxis** are fast, convenient and generally lower priced than in other major urban areas. Avoid unmarked cabs or any limousines that try to solicit service.
- If your explorations will be limited to downtown Washington, then it's best to travel by Metro. However, if you'll be traveling to outlying areas or nearby cities, a **rental car** may be your best bet.
- All airports have several **car rental companies** on site; however, it's wise to reserve your car in advance. Ask for discounts or inexpensive upgrades when you arrive.

Ronald Reagan Washington National Airport

Washington's busiest airport lies 4 miles (6.5km) south of the city on the Virginia side of the Potomac (tel: 703/417-8000).

- **Taxis** ($$) are fast, convenient and reasonably priced since the city is close by. Virginia cabs charge by the meter, D.C. cabs charge by zones, but there's little difference in the totals.
- **SuperShuttle** ($$) offers door-to-door service from the airport. Fares are flat fee per person, additional passengers pay less (tel: 800/258-3826).
- **Metro** ($) blue and yellow lines run from Ronald Reagan Washington National Airport to downtown D.C. The Metro stops next to terminals B and C Mon–Thu 5am–midnight, Fri–Sat and holidays 7am–3am, Sun 7am–midnight (tel: 202/637-7000).
- **If you drive,** take George Washington Memorial Parkway north along the Potomac River. There are four bridges that cross the river into downtown D.C. The fourth one, Theodore Roosevelt Bridge, leads directly onto Constitution Avenue and the National Mall.

Washington Dulles International Airport

This gleaming futuristic airport is becoming ever more busy, although it lies 26 miles (42km) from downtown Washington (tel: 703/572-2700).

- **Taxis** ($$$$) from Dulles can be fast and convenient but expensive because of the distance from downtown D.C.
- **SuperShuttle** ($$–$$$) offers door-to-door service from the airport to wherever you're going. Quoted fares apply to single riders; additional passengers usually pay less than half fare (tel: 800/258-3826).

- **The Washington Flyer** ($$) is a bus service between Washington Dulles and Ronald Reagan Washington National airports. There's also service between Washington Dulles Airport and West Falls Church Metro Station. The buses leaves every half hour and each trip takes about 45 minutes.
- **If you drive,** take the Dulles Airport Highway to I-66 and Washington. Follow I-66 across the Potomac on Theodore Roosevelt Bridge, which leads directly onto Constitution Avenue and the National Mall.

Baltimore-Washington International Airport (BWI)

BWI offers efficient train service into the city (tel: 410/859-7100).
- **Taxis** ($$$$) can be fast and convenient, but fairly pricey as the airport is a solid hour's drive from downtown D.C. (longer at rush hour).
- **SuperShuttle** ($$–$$$) offers door-to-door service from the airport to wherever you're going. Quoted fares apply to single riders; additional passengers pay less than half fare (tel: 800/258-3826).
- **Amtrak** and **MARC** ($$)offer regular service to Union Station.
- **If you drive,** take I-95 south to the Capital Beltway (I-495). For downtown Washington, take the Beltway north to I-66 east, cross the Theodore Roosevelt Bridge and exit onto Constitution Avenue.

Tourism Offices

For telephone inquiries or to order visitor information, contact the Washington D.C. Convention and Tourism Corporation, 901 7th Street N.W., Fourth Floor, Washington DC 20001, tel: 202/789-7000; www.washington.org
- There are **National Park Service information kiosks** at the Vietnam Veterans Memorial (► 84–85) and at several other locations throughout the city.

Getting Around

The Metro (Subway)

Built at a cost of over $10 billion, Washington's subway system is clean, fast, efficient and one of the safest in the country. It should be your first choice for getting around the city.

Getting From Here to There on the Metro

The Washington Metro Area Transit Authority (WMATA) offers an excellent brochure *(A Metro Guide to the Nation's Capital),* which has a map of the Metro system and lists all of the Metro subway lines and bus numbers for the city's major attractions (see inside front cover). For more WMATA information, tel: 202/637-7000; www.wmata.com

Buying and Using a Fare Card

The Metro does not accept cash or tokens. You must purchase a fare card from the automated machines just inside the entrance before entering the boarding area.
- **Fare card machines** accept coins, bills, ATM cards and credit cards.

Metro Hours of Operation
Mon–Thu 5am–midnight, Fri–Sat and holidays 7am–3am,
Sun 7am–midnight

- You can purchase a **one-day unlimited-use** fare card for $6.50.
- The machines can only return a maximum of $5 in change. On weekdays the card can only be used after 9:30am
- Insert your card, arrow first, into the slot of the turnstile. The card will pop up on top of the turnstile. **Take it with you** – you'll need it to exit at the next station.
- Continue using the fare card until its value drops below the minimum ride fare rate, then buy a new card. The balance remaining from the first card can be redeemed in the "**Used Fare Card Trade-In**" slot in the fare card machine.
- Follow the signs to the **platform** for your subway. To make sure you get on the right train, headed in the right direction, check the destination that appears on the train.

Buses

Bus services, operated by WMATA, can be a handy alternative to areas not serviced by Metro, particularly Georgetown. WMATA offers a *Metro System Route Map* (call WMATA, 202/637-7000), which, together with the bus schedules, can help you find the right bus.

- Look for the **red, white and blue** Metro bus signs, which list the numbers of the buses that stop there.
- Metro bus fares are **inexpensive**.
- You must have the **correct change** to board.
- **Rail transfers** (obtained from Metro stations) are worth 90 cents of the fare. Get additional bus transfers from the driver as you board the bus.

Taxis

- Washington taxis do not use meters. The fare is set by the **number of zones** your route takes you through. There are eight zones in the city. There are additional **small charges** for extra luggage, rush-hour transit and services that take the driver away from the cab.
- Always get the **driver's name** or the **license number** of any cab you ride in so that the cab can be identified if you inadvertently leave something behind, or if you have a complaint. If you do have complaints or think you might have been overcharged, call the D.C. Taxicab Commission (tel: 202/645-6018).

Walking

Washington is a beautiful city and parts of it are ideal for walking.

- The **downtown** area, including the National Mall, Capitol Hill, the Federal District, the White House vicinity and Foggy Bottom, is user-friendly and well-policed.
- The large **Northwest quadrant** of the city has many neighborhoods that are great for exploring on foot, including Georgetown, Adams-Morgan and Dupont Circle. There are some questionable pockets here and there, so some discretion is advised.
- The areas northeast and southeast of the Capitol and south of I-395, contain a **mixed bag** of neighborhoods, including many that are rundown and some that are dangerous for visitors. Avoid exploring these areas on foot.

Car Rental

There are many rental-car companies operating throughout the city and at the airports.

- It's a good idea to **reserve** a car ahead of time, as it can sometimes be difficult to find a car on short notice, particularly at the airports.

Most car rental companies charge a **flat per-day rate** that includes unlimited mileage, but verify such details before signing any papers. There will be **additional charges** for insurance and for filling the gas tank when you return the car (unless you've filled it yourself just before bringing it back).

You may be offered an **upgrade** from, say, economy to a midsize car at a very reasonable rate.

Car Rental Companies
Avis (tel: 800/331-1212)
Budget (tel: 800/527-0700)
Dollar (tel: 800/800-4000)
Hertz (tel: 800/654-3131)
National (tel: 800/227-7368)

Driving Tips

City traffic, which can vary from light to heavy at any time of the day, usually becomes gridlocked during **rush hours** (7–9am and 4–6:30pm). Avoid driving at these times.

Seat belts must be worn at all times.

Turning right on a red light after a full stop is often allowed, but in every case check whether signage limits or forbids this, especially at many of the city's busier intersections.

Unless otherwise posted, the **speed limit** on city streets is 25mph (40kph). D.C. police often stop speeders, particularly in residential areas.

Parking garages tend to fill early on weekdays, and street parking downtown is often nonexistent after 9am If you park on the street, check the signage to make sure you are parking legally. If you park illegally, your car may be towed. If that happens, phone 202/727-5000 (or visit www.dmv.dc.gov to find out where it is and how to get it back).

Train Stations

Union Station is the primary train station for Washington, D.C. and has a very convenient central location, within walking distance of Capitol Hill and most of the Smithsonian museums.

Amtrak offers fast rail service from Washington to New York (2.5 hours).

A **Metro station** at Union Station offers connections throughout the city.

Orienting Yourself

The city is divided into four quadrants – Northeast, Northwest, Southeast and Southwest – with the Capitol in the center.

Streets running north and south are **numbered**, beginning with 1st Street at the Capitol.

East–west streets have **letters**.

Most angled streets are named after **states**.

important info,

The major east–west streets on either side of the Mall are Constitution and Independence avenues.

Admission Charges
The cost of admission to museums and places of interest mentioned in the text is indicated by the following price categories:
Inexpensive under $7 **Moderate** $7–$13 **Expensive** over $13

Washington Neighborhoods

- **Downtown** generally refers to the area from Capitol Hill to the Potomac River, which includes the National Mall, federal buildings, the White House and surrounding business district. Approximate boundaries are D Street S.W. to the south and G Street N.W. to the north.
- **The Mall** is a narrower slice of downtown, including the large central expanse of lawn along with the monuments and museums that lie between Independence and Constitution avenues, and between the Capitol and the Potomac River.
- **Foggy Bottom** lies between the White House and the Potomac River.
- **Georgetown,** one of Washington's oldest neighborhoods, is bounded by the Potomac River to the south, Georgetown University to the west and Rock Creek Park to the east.
- **Dupont Circle** includes the streets surrounding Dupont Circle and extends northwest, where it borders Adams-Morgan.
- **Adams-Morgan** is bounded by Rock Creek Park to the west, 16th Street to the east and S Street to the south.
- **Southwest, Southeast** and **Northeast** contain a wide variety of residential neighborhoods, some of which have higher-than-average crime rates. Avoid walking through neighborhoods lying northeast or south-east of Capitol Hill or south of the I-395.

Accommodations

Washington, D.C. has some of the finest and most expensive hotels in the country. Big price tags usually mean considerable pampering. Lower-end establishments will be merely functional, although with pleasant touches if you're careful to choose the best. For a small-town-in-a-big-city feeling, you could try a small inn or a bed-and-breakfast. There are also numerous moderately priced establishments that offer good service with fewer luxuries.

Location

Most hotels are located in the city's Northwest quadrant, scattered about downtown, Georgetown, the West End, Dupont Circle, Capitol Hill and Upper Northwest. But good public transportation will let you explore the city easily. Political crowds tend to stay near the White House, Capitol Hill and other government buildings downtown. Tourists usually prefer Georgetown, Dupont Circle and Upper Northwest. Georgetown doesn't have Metro access but it's only a short taxi ride away from the rest of D.C.

Reservations

Hotel rates vary greatly, depending on availability and time of year. Rates are highest when Congress is in session, during election seasons, for the Cherry Blossom Festival in late March or early April, and around graduation in late May and early June. Discounted rates can be found, especially on weekends and when Congress is not in session (Christmas and late summer). Corporate and senior rates are also usually available. Note that parking can add $20–$30 per night.

In general, small children can stay in the room at no extra cost. Residential and suite hotels are often better suited for large families. For less expensive lodgings, stay in suburban Virginia or Maryland. This guide ncludes a selection of Washington hotels in various price categories. Be sure to reserve your hotel room well in advance.

For more information, here are a few places to contact:

- **AAA Mid-Atlantic**, 701 15th Street N.W., tel: 202/331-3000, provides members with the *Mid-Atlantic TourBook*.
- **Washington D.C. Convention and Tourism Corporation,** 901 7th Street, 4th Floor, Washington DC 20001, tel: 202/789-7000; www.washington.org, can send you a list of participating hotels.
- **Bed and Breakfast Accommodations Ltd.,** Box 12011, Washington DC 20005, tel: (877) 893-3233; www.bedandbreakfastdc.com, specializes in reservations for B&Bs in the area.

Diamond Ratings

AAA's one- (♦) or two- (♦♦) diamond rating represents a clean and well-maintained property offering comfortable rooms, with the two-diamond property showing enhancements in decor and furnishings. A three (♦♦♦) diamond property shows marked upgrades in physical attributes, services and comfort and may offer additional amenities. A four (♦♦♦♦) diamond rating signifies a property offering a high level of service and hospitality and a wide variety of amenities and upscale facilities. A five- (♦♦♦♦♦) diamond rating represents a world-class facility, offering the highest level of luxurious accommodations and personalized guest services.

List of Places To Stay

Following is a selective list of some of the city's best lodging. Rates may vary significantly if rooms are reserved through a travel agent or are discounted. Most standard chains in the hotel industry (not listed here) have hotels in Washington, D.C. Check with individual hotels about wheelchair access and the extent of their facilities for people with disabilities.

Prices
Prices are the minimum for a double room during high season, excluding 14.5 percent lodging tax:
$ under $160 **$$** $160–$260 **$$$** over $260

♦♦♦ Churchill Hotel $$

Near Dupont Circle, this hotel offers the largest rooms of any hotel in Washington, with notable extra touches. The staff are very attentive to your every need. Step out your door and you're next to the best restaurants and shops.

🏛 197 E3 ✉ 1914 Connecticut Avenue N.W. ☎ 202/797-2000 or 800/424-2464; www.thechurchillhotel.com

♦♦♦ Dupont at the Circle $$

Each of the nine rooms at this intimate bed-and-breakfast establishment is individually decorated, and many have Victorian stained-glass windows, decorative fireplaces, antique and brass beds, and clawfooted or Jacuzzi tub. Continental breakfast is served in the 19th-century dining room. This inn is only one block off Dupont Circle.

🏛 197 F2 ✉ 1604–1606 19th Street at Q Street N.W. ☎ 202/332-5251 or (888) 412-0100; www.dupontatthecircle.com

♦♦♦♦ Four Seasons Hotel Washington $$$

No Washington establishment offers better service – staff members know you by name, a concierge is available 24 hours, a complimentary town car is available for nearby service, and there are many more amenities. The luxurious rooms and suites match state-of-the-art technology with the richest comforts. The health club is the city's finest.

197 D1 2800 Pennsylvania Avenue at M Street N.W. 202/342-0444; fax 202/342-1673; www.fourseasons.com

Hay-Adams $$$

With a dazzling view of the White House and Lafayette Park, the Hay-Adams has Washington's premier address. Built in Italian Renaissance style, the boutique hotel exudes Old World grandeur and offers formal service. Consider an intimate meal in the hotel's Lafayette restaurant. There also is an evening champagne bar with piano music, where it is not uncommon to rub shoulders with at least a few political celebrities.

194 C4 1 Lafayette Square N.W. 202/638-6600 or 800/424-5054; fax 202/638-2716; www.hayadams.com

Courtyard by Marriott-Embassy Row $

Completely renovated in 2006, this modern boutique hotel offers fine bedding and comfortable furnishings, as well as heated indoor pool and spa. On Scott Circle, the hotel is close to three Metro Stations and within walking distance of the White House, Connecticut Avenue and Dupont Circle.

194 B5 1600 Rhode Island Avenue N.W. 202/293-8000; fax: 202/293-0085; www.courtyardembassyrow.com

Henley Park Hotel $

An easy walk to Metro Center and Gallery Place Metro stations, this hotel, with its Tudor-style halls and rooms, also is close to the MCI Arena and Washington Convention Center. Services include evening turndown, plush spa robes, shoe shine, morning newspaper and sedan service. The hotel's American-style restaurant is among the city's best.

195 D5 926 Massachusetts Avenue N.W. 202/638-5200 or 800/222-8474; fax 202/638-6740; www.henleypark.com

Hilton Washington Embassy Row $

This small, European-style boutique hotel has spacious rooms and a convenient location at Dupont Circle on the prestigious Embassy Row. The Smithsonian museums, monuments, White House and Kennedy Center are all nearby, as is the nightlife of Dupont Circle and Georgetown.

197 E2 2015 Massachusetts Avenue N.W. 202/265-1600; fax: 202/328-7526; www.hiltonembassyrow.com

Hotel George $$

This contemporary hotel offers a refreshing departure from the stalwart Old World-style hotels that characterize much of Washington. Rooms have oversize executive desks, cordless phones, interactive cable TV and DVD systems with environmental sounds. Bistro Bis (➤ 156), the hotel's French-inspired restaurant, is a must for dinner.

200 B4 15 E Street N.W. 202/347-4200 or 800/576-8331; www.hotelgeorge.com

Hotel Washington $$

This landmark 1918 hotel has a spectacular view of the White House and the Washington Monument. The rooftop restaurant and bar opens May through October. Rooms have luxurious linens, mahogany furniture and marble bathrooms. The National Theatre is also close by.

194 C4 515 15th Street N.W. 202/638-5900; fax 202/638-4275; www.hotelwashington.com

Jurys Normandy $

Five blocks off Dupont Circle, the Normandy houses small, cozy rooms with two-post beds. Each has a coffeemaker, refrigerator, hair dryer, in-room safe and high-speed internet.

Continental breakfast is served daily, and coffee and tea are set out in the afternoon. The hotel's attention to guests' needs is impressive.

🔲 197 E3 ✉ 2118 Wyoming Avenue at Connecticut Avenue N.W. ☎ 202/483-1350 or 800/424-3729; fax 202/387-8241; www.jurysdoyle.com

▾▾▾ Latham Hotel $$

This charming hotel near the C&O Canal in Georgetown combines European-style elegance with comfort. Small, refined rooms with palewood furniture all have modern conveniences; the Carriage Suites have upstairs bedrooms. The Latham has Georgetown's only outdoor swimming pool. Michel Richard's Citronelle (▶ 101) is one of the country's best French restaurants.

🔲 196 C1 ✉ 3000 M Street N.W. ☎ 202/726-5000 or (888) 587-2377; fax 202/337-4250; www.thelatham.com

▾▾▾ Morrison-Clark Inn $

Two 19th-century town homes became this hotel. Antiques fill the public rooms, where fireplaces glow in winter. Decor ranges from Victorian to provincial French to neoclassical. The restaurant offers regional American cuisine.

🔲 195 D5 ✉ 1015 L Street N.W. near Massachusetts Avenue ☎ 202/898-1200 or 800/222-8474; fax 202/289-8576; www.morrisonclark.com

▾▾▾ Hotel Rouge $$

This trendy luxury boutique hotel located on Embassy Row near Dupont Circle offers daring red accents throughout. The contemporary lobby is accented with glass sculptures, and the red carpeted hallways lead to 137 modern guestrooms with mood lighting, speaker phones and high-speed internet.

🔲 194 C5 ✉ 1315 16th Street, NW ☎ 202/232-8000; www.rougehotel.com

▾▾ Phoenix Park Hotel $$

Named after a park in Dublin, the Phoenix Park is famous for its spirited Dubliner pub (▶ 158).

The individually decorated bedrooms have a Georgian Revival theme and vary in size. The friendly hotel is across the street from Union Station.

🔲 200 B4 ✉ 520 N. Capitol Street at Massachusetts Avenue N.W. ☎ 202/638-6900 or 800/824-5419; www.phoenixparkhotel.com

▾▾▾▾ Renaissance Mayflower Hotel $$

Listed on the National Register of Historic Places, this hotel has seen presidential inaugural balls, visiting royalty and foreign dignitaries. The lobby has gilded ceilings with bas-relief carvings, and chandeliers and marble. Rooms are elegant with modern furnishings, Italian linens and high-speed internet access. The Mayflower is within easy walking distance of Dupont Circle.

🔲 197 F1 ✉ 1127 Connecticut Avenue N.W. ☎ 202/347-3000 or 800/228-7697; fax 202/466-9083; www.renaissancemayflower.com

▾▾▾▾ Willard Inter-Continental Washington $$$

Two blocks from the White House, the Willard InterContinental has hosted numerous U.S. presidents and foreign leaders. Martin Luther King, Jr. wrote his "I Have a Dream" speech here. It is the hotel favored by most lobbyists in their quest to influence politicians.

🔲 194 C4 ✉ 1401 Pennsylvania Avenue N.W. ☎ 202/628-9100 or 800/327-0200; fax 202/637-7326; www.washington.intercontinental.com

▾▾▾ Wyndham Washington, D.C. $$

This 14-story hotel has a beautiful atrium lobby and offers comfort, quality service, and luxurious bedding in the spacious rooms. It is within walking distance of the White House, Smithsonian museums, the Convention Center and Georgetown.

🔲 194 C5 ✉ 1400 M Street N.W. ☎ 202/429-1700, fax: 202/758-0786; www.wyndham.com

...g and Drink

...ington has some of the country's finest restaurants serving every type ...cuisine. Restaurants near the White House and U.S. Capitol focus on power lunches, while establishments in Dupont Circle and Upper Northwest are busiest at dinner.

Guide to Neighborhoods

Within one block of Columbia Road and 18th Street N.W. in **Adams-Morgan**, there's a concentration of ethnic restaurants ranging from Ethiopian to French Indian, Turkish and more. A number of commendable new American and ethnic restaurants, many with outdoor terraces, line Connecticut Avenue in **Woodley Park**.

Chinatown, surrounding 6th and G streets N.W., is where you'll find the majority of Chinese, Thai and other Asian restaurants.

The city's fashionable **Dupont Circle** neighborhood offers a number of good ethnic restaurants and cafés. In **Georgetown** and the **West End**, you'll find every type of establishment, from some of the city's top restaurants to its cheapest joints.

The area surrounding the **White House** is populated with business and government workers. A number of the city's most expensive restaurants are located here, catering to generous expense accounts. Understandably for its location, **Capitol Hill** has a number of restaurants crowded with government workers and lobbyists at lunch, but which are usually quiet at night.

Reserving a Table

Reservations are essential at most of Washington's restaurants, especially for weekday lunches and weekend dinners. Usually you won't need to call more than a day in advance.

Less Expensive Options

If you want to check out a high-end restaurant but lack the cash, consider lunch instead of dinner; in many restaurants lunch can often cost a third less than dinner because the restaurant is less busy. Some establishments offer inexpensive pre-theater menus as well.

Recommended Places To Eat and Drink

Each of the chapters in this book has a listing of recommended places to eat and drink. They are listed alphabetically, and price guidelines are displayed. The sales tax in Washington, D.C. is 10 percent, and tipping is expected at 15 to 20 percent of the bill.

Credit Cards

Credit cards are the normal method of payment in restaurants (the cards accepted should be clearly indicated – usually American Express, Diners Club, Discover, MasterCard or Visa). If in any doubt, check before you order. Some of the less expensive cafés, bars and delis only accept cash.

Prices
The $ symbol indicates what you can expect to pay for an average, complete dinner for one person, including drinks, tax and tip:
$ under $30 **$$** $30–$60 **$$$** over $60

Late-Night Dining

Washington has fewer late-night dining options than some other big U.S. cities.

- For something upscale, try **Les Halles** (➤ 72).
- For something intellectual, try **Kramerbooks & Afterwards Café** (➤ 130).
- For something casual, consider the **Bistro Français** (➤ 125).

Bests...
...breakfast: Old Ebbitt Grill (➤ 72)
...coffee atmosphere: Teaism (➤ 73)
...French: The Bistro Bis (➤ 156)
...Indian: Bombay Club (➤ 101)
...Japanese: Sushi-Ko (➤ 128)
...power lunch: Palm (➤ 127)
...romantic dinner: 1789 (➤ 128)
...seafood: Sea Catch (➤ 128)
...scene: D.C. Coast (➤ 71)
...steak: The Prime Rib (➤ 103)
...wine and food experience: Equinox (➤ 101)

Shopping

The best shopping neighborhoods are Dupont Circle, Georgetown and Upper Northwest near Friendship Heights.

Further Information

Check the Style section of *The Washington Post* for its fashion reports, *Washingtonian* magazine for haute couture news and the *Washington City Paper* for advertisements. Try the *Yellow Pages* for quirky items.

Prices

Except at the Eastern Market weekend flea market, where vendors will readily bargain, prices are usually non-negotiable. "Going out of business, everything must go" is often a scam. Sales tax is an additional six percent.

Opening Hours

Store hours vary widely, with some closing at 6pm and others – particularly in bustling Georgetown and Dupont Circle – staying open later. Many stores remain open late on Thursdays and are open on Sundays.

Clothing

You will find **designer clothing** at Georgetown Park, the city's best shopping mall, as well as in the various shops lining M Street in Georgetown.

The **best department stores,** all in Upper Northwest near Friendship Heights, are Lord & Taylor, Neiman Marcus and Saks Fifth Avenue. Head to Dupont Circle for **top trendy wear** and to Adams-Morgan for **funkier, alternative apparel.**

Art

Dupont Circle (R Street N.W.) and Georgetown (M Street N.W.) are the city's art neighborhoods, housing the majority of galleries.

Bests...
...**antiques:** Susquehanna (➤ 130)
...**bookstore:** Kramerbooks (➤ 131)
...**bread:** Marvelous Market (➤ 131)
...**flea market:** Eastern Market (➤ 155)
...**foodie market:** Dean & DeLuca (➤ 131)
...**funky neighborhood to explore:** Adams-Morgan (➤ 131)
...**housewares:** Home Rule (➤ 131)
...**museum store:** National Gallery of Art (➤ 54–58)
...**new designer for women:** Betsey Johnson (➤ 130)
...**shoes:** Shake Your Booty (➤ 131)

Entertainment

Washington's reputation for fine theater, dance and music has blossomed over the past two decades, with the John F. Kennedy Center for the Performing Arts firmly at the center of the capital's cultural scene in entertainment.

- At the John F. Kennedy Center (➤ 132) you will find the **Washington Opera, Ballet** and **National Symphony Orchestra (NSO)**, as well as family theater, modern dance performances, drama and musicals.
- Washington has nearly 50 professional **theaters** hosting everything from Broadway productions to offbeat plays and poetry readings.
- A number of **concert halls** focus on classical, jazz and pop music.
- Some museums and galleries, like the National Museum of American History (➤ 62–64) and National Gallery of Art (➤ 54–58), host **free seasonal music concerts**.
- The Kennedy Center's Millennium Stage has **free daily concerts** at 6pm

Information and Reservations
Reserve ahead, if possible, for concerts, musicals and plays. With the opera, last-minute cancellations may free up some seats. But there's so much happening, you're bound to find something to entertain you.
- Phone or visit a theater's **box office** (generally open from noon until showtime) – you might score same-day tickets for a hit show.

Ticket Agencies
- **Ticketmaster:** tel: 202/397-7328 or 800/551-7328 for seats to most plays, concerts and other events. Surcharge; no refunds or exchanges.
- **TicketPlace:** tel: 202/842-5387. Half-price, same-day tickets for selected events. Phone for a list of performances or go to 407 7th Street N.W. (open Tue–Fri 11–6, Sat 10–5).
- **Tickets.com:** tel: 800/955-5566. On-line reservations for Ford's Theatre, Arena Stage, Signature Theatre, the 9:30 Club and others.

Further Information
Check the Friday Weekend section and Sunday Arts section of *The Washington Post* (www.washingtonpost.com) or the Thursday Weekend section of the *Washington Times* (www.washingtontimes.com). The *Washington City Paper* and *Washingtonian* magazine (www.washingtonian.com) also detail events.

The East Mall

Getting Your Bearings

One mile (1.6km) long by 300 feet (91m) wide, the East Mall is a grassy, tree-studded expanse, laced with paths and surrounded by an unparalleled collection of galleries and museums that offers one of the world's premier cultural experiences. Several of these establishments, notably the National Gallery of Art (➤ 54–58), the National Air and Space Museum (➤ 50–53) and the National Museum of Natural History (➤ 59–61), are among the best in their class. Surrounding them is a plethora of smaller establishments that present exceptional, if more tightly focused, collections and works of art.

These museums and galleries are incredibly popular. The Air and Space Museum alone receives over 5 million visitors every year, and at times the crowds even in the quieter galleries can seem overwhelming. It's therefore nice that you can escape into the parklike green space of the Mall. Food vendors and alfresco music, courtesy of street performers, lend a festive air.

To see the highlights of the fabulous collections in these buildings in a single day is difficult. A wiser choice would be to select one or two museums and take your time enjoying their collections at a leisurely pace. Be sure to wear comfortable walking shoes, as a full circuit of the museums would involve a trek of several miles.

15TH ST NW

Inters
Comm
Commis

National
Museum of
American
History

JEFF

INDEPEND

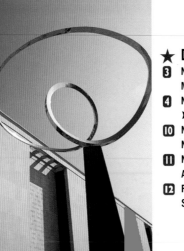

★ Don't Miss

3 National Air and Space Museum ➤ 50

4 National Gallery of Art ➤ 54

10 National Museum of Natural History ➤ 59

11 National Museum of American History ➤ 62

12 Freer and Arthur M. Sackler Galleries ➤ 65

Page 45: One of the stunning galleries at the Air and Space Museum

Below: Outdoor sculpture on the East Mall

At Your Leisure

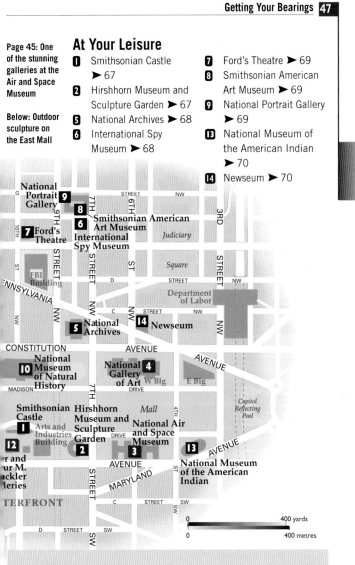

The Smithsonian: A Primer

The Smithsonian comprises 19 museums and 9 research centers. The most popular on the East Mall are the National Museum of Natural History (➤ 59–61), National Air and Space Museum (➤ 50–53), National Museum of American History (➤ 62–63), National Museum of the American Indian (➤ 70), Smithsonian Castle (➤ 67), Hirshhorn Museum (➤ 67–68), Freer and Arthur M. Sackler Galleries (➤ 65–66). Off the Mall, they include the National Portrait Gallery (➤ 69–70), the National Postal Museum (➤ 152–153), the Smithsonian American Art Museum (➤ 69), the Renwick Gallery (➤ 115), the National Zoological Park (➤ 119–120) and the Anacostia Museum (➤ 154).

You can't explore all of the East Mall in two days, but you can visit the highlights. Expect an overwhelming experience!

The East Mall in Two Days

Day One

Morning

The information hall in the **1** **Smithsonian Castle** (► 67) opens at 8:30am Here you will find displays on each of the Smithsonian museums, which can help you plan your visit. Walk east and beat the crowds by being first in line at the **3** **National Air and Space Museum** (right, ► 50–53). This open, airy museum invites a relatively breezy walk-through. The best and easiest place for lunch is Cascade Café (► 58) in the National Gallery of Art's lower level.

Afternoon

There's no way you can see more than a fraction of the fabulous collection at the **4** **National Gallery of Art** (below, ► 54–58) in just a couple of hours, but some of the must-sees include Botticelli's *Adoration of the Magi*, Rembrandt's *Saskia*, Rubens' *Daniel in the Lions' Den*, and the superb collection of French Impressionist works. Walk across to the **5** **National Archives** (► 68) for a look at the documents on which America was founded: the Declaration of Independence, the Constitution and the Bill of Rights. The building is an architectural delight, too.

Evening

Dine at 701 Pennsylvania Avenue (► 72) (reserve ahead), on modern Continental cuisine before a show. Choose from the warm Americana of **7** **Ford's Theatre** (► 69), drama at the **Arena Stage** (► 74) or the Bard's classics at the **Shakespeare Theatre** (► 74) (order tickets in advance).

Day Two

Morning

Beat the crowds into the **⑩ National Museum of Natural History** (► 59–61). The original "Teddy" bear at the museum (right) was probably named for President Theodore Roosevelt. Be sure to visit the Fossil and Dinosaur Hall and the Gem and Mineral Hall. Kids will probably enjoy the live insects in the Insect Zoo. Hit the Atrium Café (► 61) early for lunch (it gets very crowded by noon) or walk one long block north along 12th Street to check out the wonderfully diverse food court at the Old Post Office Pavilion.

Afternoon

Walk one block west to visit the **⑪ National Museum of American History** (► 62), which will reopen in 2008 with a new Star-Spangled Banner display in addition to the very popular America on the Move and American Presidency exhibits. Walk back across the Mall to the **Smithsonian Castle** (below, ► 67), where you can rest your feet for a few minutes in the pretty garden by the south entrance. So many galleries, so little time! Start half a block to the west, at the **⑫ Freer Gallery of Art** (► 65). From there, a lower-level hallway leads to the **⑫ Arthur M. Sackler Gallery** (► 66).

Evening

When you're ready for dinner, walk or take a short cab ride to enjoy the trendy Latin-Caribbean cuisine of Café Atlantico at 8th and E streets N.W. (► 71) (reservations recommended). If it's Friday or Saturday and razor-sharp political comedy is your thing, take in **Capitol Steps** at the Ronald Reagan Building and International Trade Center on Pennsylvania Avenue (► 74) (shows at 7:30pm; purchase tickets in advance).

3

National Air and Space Museum

The National Air and Space Museum's awesome display traces the history of man's passion for flight, from *Kitty Hawk* to the Space Shuttle, and is enormously popular with kids. Every year, more than 10 million people come here to view the superb historic aircraft, spacecraft and hundreds of related displays, making this the most visited museum in the world. In gallery after gallery, gleaming planes rest impressively on the ground, or hang in simulated flight suspended from the ceilings. Here you'll find the Wright Brothers' 1903 flyer as well as the *Spirit of St. Louis,* which carried Charles Lindbergh on his historic trans-Atlantic flight in 1927.

Perhaps the most impressive thing about the Air and Space Museum is that the majority of its collection spans just over 100 years. With aircraft ranging from Otto Lilienthal's 1894 glider, which influenced the Wright Brothers, to the *Voyager* spacecraft, the collection will impress you with a sense of how far aviation technology has come in just over a century.

The entrance to the museum is centrally located on the Mall (north) side of the building. It leads directly into the **Milestones of Flight Gallery**, where the museum has concentrated some of its most popular exhibits. Here, beside Charles

The National Air and Space Museum attracts more than 10 million visitors annually

The *Spirit of St. Louis* carried solo aviator Charles Lindbergh across the Atlantic in 1927

Lindbergh's *Spirit of St. Louis,* are Chuck Yeager's Bell X-1, John Glenn's *Mercury* spacecraft and the Mars Viking Lander. The most popular display is the touchable moon rock, a small chunk from the hundreds of pounds brought back by *Apollo 17.* One of the newest additions to this gallery is Spaceship 1, built by Burt Rutan, which successfully flew into sub-orbit in 2005, opening the doors of space for individuals and private enterprise.

The Milestones of Flight Gallery opens on a concourse that runs the length of the building. To your right galleries detail the history of flight. To your left they highlight the exploration of space. Nearby is the entrance to the popular **IMAX Theater** (fee charged).

Scheduled to reopen in the summer of 2008, the museum's largest gallery will host **America by Air**, presenting the history of commercial flight from the early days to the jet age. Featured aircraft include the famed Ford Tri-Motor and a Douglas DC-3, along with a walk-through forward fuselage of a Boeing 747 and a simulated

The National Air and Space Museum is noted for its collection of space suits and vehicles

Vital Statistics
- Built: 1975
- Exterior: 280,000sq ft (25,200sq m) of Tennessee pink cedar marble
- Cost: $40 million
- Record One-Day Attendance: 118,437 (April 14, 1984)

Below: The Space Race Gallery has a collection of Soviet and American rockets

flight deck of an Airbus A320 that will let visitors try their hand at "taking off" from Reagan International Airport.

On the second floor, the museum's most popular display is the Wright Brothers **Wright Flyer** the legendary wood-and-fabric plane in which they made their historic first flights. The gallery's displays also highlight the brothers' lives and flying adventures. Also on the second floor, The Great War in the Air and the World War II Aviation galleries relate the history of military aviation.

In the ultra-cool **Space Exploration** part of the museum, the large Space Race Gallery has a chilling collection of American and Russian ICBM missiles as well as the more hopeful *Apollo-Soyuz* spacecraft, whose docking, on July 17, 1975, marked a major thawing of the Cold War.

On the second-floor balcony of this gallery, you may need to wait in line to get a glimpse inside the 48-foot (14m) **Skylab Orbital**

Workshop. This unit was built as a backup of the original, which housed American astronauts and researchers for up to three months at a time.

Across the hall, the museum's most popular gallery, **From Apollo to the Moon**, traces America's eight-year challenge to land a man on the moon issued by President John F. Kennedy in 1961. Among its exhibits are the *Apollo 11* command module, *Columbia*, and the Lunar Rover, a copy of the buggylike vehicle that carried men across the surface of the moon.

The museum's only downsides are a result of its enormous popularity. It can be crowded, particularly at midday, when how much you see may depend on how much jostling and noise you can stand. On the positive side, the museum has improved its interactivity in hands-on areas like the How Things Fly gallery and with exhibits like the Flight Simulator Zone, which lets you climb into simulators and experience flying in aircraft from Top Gun jets to the **Spirit of St. Louis**. Also, this is one of the few national museums where seeing the highlights takes a relatively short time. View the Milestones of Flight and From Apollo to the Moon galleries, and you will have seen the best the museum has to offer. Breezing through the museum's 20 or so other galleries will take you about three hours.

Above: One of the most successful airplanes of all time is the Douglas DC-3

TAKING A BREAK

The **Wright Place Food Court** offers above-average cafeteria food in a geodesic glass enclosure with an exceptional view across to the Capitol.

➕ 195 E2 ✉ Independence Avenue at 4th Street S.W. ☎ 202/633-1000; www.nasm.si.edu 🕐 Daily 10–5:30; closed Dec 25. Guided tours 10:30 and 1 🎫 Free 🍴 Wright Place Food Court $ 🚇 L'Enfant Plaza, Smithsonian

NATIONAL AIR AND SPACE MUSEUM: INSIDE INFO

Top tip The museum can get uncomfortably crowded at times. To **beat the crowds**, arrive between 9:30 and 10am or after 4pm

Hidden gem For years, the Air and Space Museum had room to display only a small part of its vast collection of historic aircraft. This changed with the opening of the Udvar Hazy Center in 2003. The Center, 40 miles (64.5km) from downtown Washington at the Dulles International Airport, is housed in a 760,000sq foot (68,400sq m) hangar-shape museum, with room for the Space Shuttle *Enterprise* and a sleek, black Lockheed SR-71 spyplane. All told there are more than 100 aircraft and dozens of space artifacts on display, including biplanes, airliners, helicopters, rockets and satellites. A shuttle bus ($12) runs between the museums at 9am, 1am, noon, 1:30pm, 3pm and 5pm (schedule may vary).

❹

National Gallery of Art

In part, Washingtonians have Catherine the Great and Joseph Stalin to thank for the treasures housed here. Andrew Mellon, the industrialist and financier who founded the gallery, owned only the finest and most historically important works, and his philosophy continues to this day. The displays form one of the world's largest and most impressive collections of European and American art. Mellon's original gift of 121 artworks formed the core collection, many of which came from the Hermitage in Russia, works originally collected by Catherine the Great and sold to Mellon in the 1930s by cash-hungry Stalinists.

In addition to his fabulous art collection, Andrew Mellon also gave Washington a spectacular building to put it in. Designed by John Russell Pope (who also designed the Jefferson Memorial), the National Gallery of Art building is itself a work of art. A broad sweep of marble stairs leads through heavy bronze doors into the dramatically beautiful rotunda. Here, massive black marble pillars rise to the domed roof, defining a spacious open area with a cascading fountain at its center.

The Adoration of the Magi by Sandro Botticelli dates from 1481

The serene
Alba Madonna
by Raphael

Two great halls run east and west from the central rotunda.
They do double duty, serving as a display area for some of the
sculptures and also offering rows of open doorways that
beckon you into a veritable labyrinth of gallery rooms.

The size and scope of the collection are truly mind-boggling.
The **West Building** is the oldest and largest part of the museum
and contains all but the 20th-century works. With more than
100 gallery rooms on the main floor and still more on the lower
level, it is impossible to see the entire collection in a single day.
In room after room, masterpieces hang in profusion. The names
of the artists roll off the tongue like a Who's Who of great
masters: Botticelli, El Greco and Raphael; Rubens, Rembrandt
and Gainsborough. And then there are the Impressionists –
Monet, Renoir, Van Gogh and Cassatt – and the Post-
Impressionist Cézanne, to name just a few.

In the 1940s, the gallery was running out of space for its
collection. It also desperately needed room to begin displaying
a growing collection of 20th-century artists. The Chinese-
American architect I. M. Pei – known for designing famous
buildings in Dallas, London and Hong Kong, the JFK Library
in Boston, and the extraordinary steel-and-glass pyramid
entrance to the Louvre in Paris – was contracted to design
a new wing for the museum that would be built on the
irregularly shaped plot of land just east of the gallery. The
resulting East Building is a dramatic departure from the
Federalist architecture that dominates the Mall. Its open, airy
spaces and complex geometric shapes both contrast with and
complement the museum's West Building, and offer a stunning

environment in which to display the museum's exceptional collection of 20th-century paintings and sculptures.

An **underground concourse** connects the two parts of the gallery, and also houses a colorful museum shop and a bright café with a wall of glass that looks directly into a tumbling waterfall.

Highlights of the Collection

13th- to 15th-Century Italian (Rooms 1 to 15)

The paintings in these rooms are among the gallery's oldest. Many depict the Madonna and Child and other biblical scenes. The earliest work is Byzantine, but the later works show a steady transition to the naturalistic style of the Renaissance. The movement of free-flowing lines is evident in Botticelli's luminous *Adoration of the Magi*. Here too is the only painting by Leonardo da Vinci displayed outside Europe, his melancholy and haunting portrait of *Ginevra de'Benci*.

16th-Century Italian and Spanish (Rooms 16 to 28)

With the Renaissance in full swing, the exploration of artistic styles spread to many Italian cities. In these rooms you'll find superb examples of the work of Italian masters from Florence and Venice, including Titian's magnificent *St. John the Evangelist on Patmos*. Here too is one of Andrew Mellon's original purchases from the Hermitage Museum in Russia, Raphael's serene *Alba Madonna*.

17th-Century Dutch and Flemish (Rooms 42 to 50)

If you're looking for Dutch and Flemish masters, you'll find excellent examples of their works in these rooms. Here Vermeer's *Woman Holding a Balance* and Rembrandt's mysterious portrait of his wife, *Saskia*, present visual essays in shadow and light. But by far the most arresting masterpiece here is Peter Paul Rubens' large, sumptuous and brawny **Daniel in the Lions' Den**.

18th- and 19th-Century British (Rooms 57 to 61)

The most eye-catching works in these rooms are the seascapes of J. M. W. Turner, which include the misty *Approach to Venice* and *Rotterdam Ferry-Boat*. Also here are works by Joshua Reynolds and Thomas Gainsborough and, strangely, *The Skater*, by American painter Gilbert Stuart, which was

Peter Paul Rubens' work *Daniel in the Lions' Den* is one of the finest examples of 17th-century art in the gallery

considered a radical departure from typical portraiture of the time, as it showed the subject engaged in a strenuous activity.

18th- and 19th-Century American (Rooms 60 and 62 to 71)

In the 18th and 19th centuries, a handful of American artists made their influence felt on the world stage. Among them was the "Father of American Portraiture," Gilbert Stuart, whose work here includes the **"Athenaeum" portrait of George Washington** (one of four portraits he painted of the first president). Stuart went on to paint portraits of the next four presidents. Among the other U.S. artists represented here are Thomas Cole, Rembrandt Peale, James Abbott McNeill Whistler and Winslow Homer.

19th-Century French (Rooms 80 to 93)

The museum's superb collection of works by French Impressionists fills these popular galleries. Here you'll find Monet's lovely *Woman with a Parasol,* Toulouse-Lautrec's strangely journalistic paintings of underground life in Paris, and Gauguin's powerful *Self-Portrait.* Other artists represented include Mary Cassatt, Vincent van Gogh and Edward Degas, whose **Four Dancers** is one of the most famous paintings in the collection. And be sure not to miss the mastery of form and light found in Renoir's *Oarsman at Chatou.*

20th Century (East Building)

The wide-open spaces and startling angular design of I. M. Pei's arresting East Building left surprisingly little space for the displaying of artwork. Often, much of the space is filled with traveling exhibits, but there's a core collection of excellent 20th-century works, including Pablo Picasso's bleak and sorrowful *The Tragedy* from his Blue Period. There are also several works by Henri Matisse, including the lively *Pianist and Checker Players,* and works by more contemporary artists from Jasper Johns to Andy Warhol.

The angular design of I. M. Pei's East Building

TAKING A BREAK

The **Cascade Café**, on the lower-level concourse, offers excellent coffee, tasty pastas and creative sandwiches. The food is some of the best on the Mall, and with views through a large glass window looking into a tumbling waterfall fountain it is a soothing place to stop.

✚ 195 E3 ✉ 6th Street and Constitution Avenue N.W. ☎ 202/737-4215; www.nga.gov ⏱ Mon–Sat 10–5, Sun 11–6; closed Jan 1 and Dec 25 Ⓜ Archives 🎟 Free

---

NATIONAL GALLERY OF ART: INSIDE INFO

Top tip At the west end of the gallery is a 6-acre (2.5ha) **Sculpture Garden**. At this quiet retreat paths lead through elegant plantings to a dozen or more major sculptures, including works by Alexander Calder, Joan Miró, Isamu Noguchi and others.

Hidden gem The **Pavilion Café** overlooks the Sculpture Garden at the west end of the gallery. Here you can enjoy a light lunch including specialty pizza, soup, sandwiches and more, indoors or out.

🔟

National Museum of Natural History

The National Museum of Natural History is everything a major science museum should be and more. For more than 150 years, Smithsonian scientists have traveled the globe to study the mysteries of the natural world, and the wonders they have collected are on display here for all to see.

The National Museum of Natural History is a feast for the eyes even on the outside

From the time you walk through the front doors and gaze up at the huge bull elephant that dominates the rotunda, the museum generates an "Indiana Jones works here" sense of wonder and excitement. The mandate of this museum is extremely broad, and its displays reflect the questions that Smithsonian scientists have asked from the beginning: What is the universe made of? Where did life originate? How did the human race develop? The magic of this museum is that it not only goes a long way to answering these questions in an entertaining manner, but it also shows how the answers, and even the questions, are still evolving.

With a total of over 120 million natural and cultural arti-facts, just a small percentage of the collection can be on display at any given time. Over the past few years, the museum has been refurbishing and upgrading its exhibits. Not surprisingly, the newer exhibits tend to be much more visually interesting and interactive. Some of the older exhibits appear a bit dated, and a few are somewhat culturally insensitive.

But in spite of this, most of the exhibits work superbly well, and many of the artifacts on display are unique in the world: the purportedly cursed Hope Diamond, Marie Antoinette's diamond earrings, a life-size model of a blue whale and more.

The National Museum of Natural History is on the north side of the Mall along Constitution Avenue between 9th and 12th streets N.W. The main entrance is on the Mall side of the museum. This is one of the largest of all the Smithsonian museums, but if you pick and choose carefully, you can see the highlights in about two to three hours.

The First Floor

By far the most popular exhibit on the first floor is the **Dinosaur Hall**. Kids especially love this area, where the fabulous reconstructed skeletons share space with lifelike, full-size models. Surrounding the Dinosaur Hall are several exhibits that examine the earliest life on the planet. Parents with children should take in the **Discovery Center**, where kids can experi-ence hands-on science, handling minerals, lifting an elephant

Setting the tone for adventure: a mounted bull African elephant dominates the museum's vast rotunda

This Devonian fish fossil is just one of the thousands of artifacts the museum uses to tell the story of Earth's history

tusk and even looking into the mouth of a crocodile. Also on the first floor, the **African Voices** exhibit looks at the cultural history of Africa, from the rise of the earliest humans to the social upheaval in modern South Africa.

The Second Floor

The large wing dominating the second floor displays the museum's collection of **minerals and rare gemstones**, evoking a deep appreciation of the beauty of minerals, both before and after they've been shaped by the hand of man. Here are magnificent natural mineral crystals of every hue. Here, too, are fabulous sapphires, emeralds, rubies and a host of other gems, including the **Hope Diamond**, the world's largest blue diamond, owned by Marie Antoinette and said to carry a curse.

Nearby is the magnificent **Hooker Emerald**, reputedly once part of a sultan's belt buckle. The owner, Janet Annenberg Hooker, donated it to the Smithsonian and helped fund a major renovation of the museum's Gem and Mineral Hall.

Also on the second floor, the unsqueamish will relish the **Insect Zoo**, with fascinating critters from around the world. Of interest, too, is the **Western Cultures** exhibit, which traces the rise of human cultures in Europe and the Mediterranean.

TAKING A BREAK

The **Atrium Café** on the museum's lower floor offers a variety of sandwiches, pizza, pastas and light lunches. Visit early or late as noontime can be quite crowded.

➕ 195 D3 ✉ 10th Street and Constitution Avenue N.W. ☎ 202/633-1000; www.mnh.si.edu 🕐 Late May–early Sep daily 10–5:30; early Sep–late May 10–7:30. Guided tours Sep–Jun Tue–Fri 10:30, 1:30 🎫 Free 🍴 Atrium Café: $ 📷 Archives

NATIONAL MUSEUM OF NATURAL HISTORY: INSIDE INFO

Top tip The **Gem and Mineral Exhibit** has its own shop on the second floor, selling mineral specimens, books, earth sciences oddities and semiprecious gems from around the world.

⓫

National Museum of American History

When it reopens after extensive renovations in July 2008, don't step through the doors of this place expecting a dry chronology of the country's past. Instead, this unique museum is more like the nation's attic, a crowded but delightful hodgepodge of artifacts from every era of American life. Like any good attic, this one offers surprises and delightful discoveries at every turn. Balloon-tire bikes stand beside hand-wringer washers, classic jukeboxes and antique farm machinery. There are one-of-a-kind items too, including George Washington's wooden teeth, the stovepipe hat Lincoln was wearing when he was assassinated, and the original Star-Spangled Banner – the 1813 flag that inspired the national anthem.

The First Floor

The surprises begin just inside the doors, where a reconstructed 19th-century general store and post office (from where you can still mail a letter) has been built in the foyer. Also here is the must-see **America on the Move**, a 26,000 square foot (2,340sq m) tribute to powered transportation and its effect on American life. The exhibit features colorful, hands-on displays that are fun for kids, and helpings of nostalgia for grown-ups. Starting with the early railroads and their impact on a horse-powered frontier, the exhibit includes 19 dioramas that capture moments in American history, shaped by transportation.

There are wonderfully restored trains, antique and classic cars, motorcycles and more, including a 1903 Winton, the first car to be driven across country; a 199-ton Southern Railway locomotive and an actual 40-foot (12m) stretch of Route 66. Also there are complementing exhibits on power machinery and maritime enterprise. For contrast, walk across to the other side of the floor to tour chef **Julia Child's Kitchen**, which she donated to the museum in 2001.

The Second Floor

One of the major goals of the museum's renovations in 2007 was to create a new home for the **Star-Spangled Banner**. This is the original flag that flew over Fort Henry during the bombardment of Baltimore in 1814, and which inspired Francis Scott Key to pen the immortal words to America's National Anthem. In

1998, the 185-year-old flag was badly deteriorating, and a long and painstaking restoration and conservation project was undertaken. The newly restored flag will be displayed in a climate-controlled room. Visitors will enter a space slightly above the flag, which is displayed horizontally, and will view it through windows. Also here will be displays that relate the story of the flag's creation, the war of 1812, the writing of the National Anthem, and the history of the flag after the war, up to and including the monumental restoration project.

The hat Lincoln was wearing when he was assassinated

Also on the Second floor, look for the **First Ladies Exhibit**, which examines the lives and often overlooked contributions to the nation by the wives of America's presidents.

The Third Floor

Restoration of the Star-Spangled Banner took six years

The Price of Freedom exhibit takes a sobering look at America's armed conflicts from the French and Indian Wars to the war in Iraq. The fascinating artifacts on display include George Washington's ceremonial sword and the chairs that Ulysses S.Grant and Robert E. Lee used during Lee's surrender. But the real story here is the in-depth look at the causes of the country's conflicts and the price paid for these wars in human and economic terms. Also here is **The American Presidency**, with artifacts from the lives of every U.S. president. It offers insights into how the roles and duties of the president have changed over two centuries. Artifacts range from a uniform worn by George Washington to Bill Clinton's saxaphone. Of particular interest is the exhibit showing how radio and television transformed the presidency.

Vital Statistics
- Total Exhibit Space: 750,000 square feet (67,500sq m)
- Approximate Number of Items in Collection: 3 million
- Approximate Number of Items on Display: 90,000

TAKING A BREAK
When the museum reopens there will be a café that offers sandwiches and light lunches as well as ice cream and desserts.

🞣 194 C3 ✉ 14th Street and Constitution Avenue N.W. ☎ 202/633-1000; www.americanhistory.si.edu 🕐 Daily 10–5:30 💵 Free 🍴 Café: $$
Ⓜ Smithsonian, Federal Triangle

NATIONAL MUSEUM OF AMERICAN HISTORY: INSIDE INFO

Top tip The museum's best exhibits are those that use its fascinating collection to reflect the growth and changes of everyday life in America. A good example is the reconstructed 1776 gunboat *Philadelphia* (below), which was recovered from the waters of Lake Champlain in 1935 and offers an interesting glimpse into the life of Revolutionary War-era soldiers.

One to miss The exhibits that work less well are those that take themselves too seriously, telling the story of American cultural development while using the museum's collection almost as an afterthought. Examples include the vague and poorly focused **American Encounters** (New Mexico history) and the rambling **Communities in a Changing Nation** (the promise of the 19th century).

12

Freer and Arthur M. Sackler Galleries

Although these two galleries have separate addresses, they're connected by an underground exhibition space. Together they form the Smithsonian's National Museum of Asian Art, representing over 56,000 works that constitute one of the finest Asian art collections in the western hemisphere.

Freer Gallery of Art

The Freer Gallery of Art contains a fascinating blend of Asian and American art

Opened in 1923, the Freer was the first Smithsonian museum dedicated solely to art. It is named for Charles Lang Freer, a railroad industrialist and passionate collector of American and Asian art. In fact, what makes the Freer particularly delightful is its unique blending of **American and Asian works**. The Asian works fill the larger gallery rooms, while the American paintings are hung in the hallways.

The collection includes more than 1,200 works by **James McNeill Whistler** (although only a handful are on display).

Whistler (1834–1903) was born in Massachusetts and classically trained in London and Paris. His artistic idea of incorporating Orientalism into his works was far ahead of his time. The **Art for Art's Sake** exhibit has some of Whistler's works, including *The White Symphony: Three Girls* (1868).

The centerpiece of the Whistler collection is the magnificent **Peacock Room**, once the dining room of a London town house, which the artist intricately decorated in a golden peacock motif. Freer was a passionate supporter of Whistler and bought virtually all of his works. He also patronized other American artists whose works he felt complemented his extensive Asian collection.

Throughout the main floor, small well-lit rooms hold an impressive array of Chinese paintings, Buddhist carvings, Persian manuscripts and ceramics. There is also a collection of hand-painted Japanese screens.

The gallery itself is a bright, airy, Renaissance-style palazzo with an open central courtyard with an elegant fountain.

Arthur M. Sackler Gallery

Opened in 1987, the Sackler Gallery was created around a donation of more than 1,000 superb Asian works collected by research physician and author Arthur M. Sackler. It is an extensive gallery filled with Asian art.

The collection includes superb early Chinese bronzes and jades. Of particular note is the exhibit entitled **Luxury Arts of the Silk Route Empire**, which highlights the art of everyday items used and traded by the cultures all along the Silk Road. There are exceptional ceramics and metalwork from Persia, India and China.

Another impressive display is the **Arts of China** with a stunning variety of jades, bronzes, Buddhist sculpture and wall paintings, glass, lacquerware, furniture and paintings spanning almost 6,000 years. Worth exploring too is the collection of Buddhist and Hindu religious figures.

The Peacock Room by American artist James McNeill Whistler was once the dining room of a London town house

TAKING A BREAK

The closest place to eat is the **café at the Hirshhorn Museum**, a half-block east of the Sackler Gallery.

✚ 195 D2 ✉ Freer Gallery: Jefferson Drive at 12th Street S.W.; Arthur M. Sackler Gallery: 1050 Independence Avenue S.W. ☎ 202/633-4880; www.asia.si.edu ⏰ Both: daily 10–5:30 💲 Free 🍴 Café: $ 🚇 Smithsonian, L'Enfant Plaza

FREER AND ARTHUR M. SACKLER GALLERIES: INSIDE INFO

Top tip Gallery 10 has a display of the works of several of Whistler's contemporaries, including a number of ethereal landscapes by Thomas Wilmer Dewing.

Hidden gem Spend a few extra minutes enjoying the sensuous naturalistic forms of the **Buddhist and Hindu carvings** in the South Asian sculpture gardens.

At Your Leisure

1 Smithsonian Castle

When English scientist James Smithson died in 1829, he left about $500,000 to the United States to create "an establishment for the increase and diffusion of knowledge." Smithson had never visited the United States, but he felt that the freedom the young country offered would make an excellent environment for the growth of "pure science." It took the American government some time to decide whether they would accept the gift and, if so, how it would be spent. The end result was the Smithsonian Castle, a Gothic-looking fantasy of turrets and spires completed in 1855. Originally the building was designed to house a museum, an art gallery and laboratories for all the scientific work of the institution. Over the years the collection has been moved to the 15 other Smithsonian museums or their research centers. Today the building serves as the administrative offices, but it also houses a comprehensive

visitor center that offers an overview of the Smithsonian's facilities.

🚩 195 D3 ✉ 1000 Jefferson Drive S.W.
☎ 202/633-1000;
www.si.edu/visit/ infocenter/sicastle.htm
🕙 Daily 8:30–5:30 💷 Free
Ⓜ Smithsonian

2 Hirshhorn Museum and Sculpture Garden

In his lifetime, financier and art collector Joseph Hirshhorn amassed over 12,000 contemporary works of art, including pieces by artists such as Willem de Kooning, Georgia O'Keeffe, Edward Hopper, Alexander Calder, Henry Moore and many

The original Smithsonian building, called "The Castle," was completed in 1855

others. In 1966, Hirshhorn donated his collection to the Smithsonian Institution. Within the museum, around 600 works of art can be seen, and scattered throughout the museum's grounds is Hirshhorn's collection of 3,000 sculptures.

🚼 195 E2 ✉ Independence Avenue at 7th Street S.W. ☎ 202/633-4674; http//hirshhorn.si.edu ⏰ Daily 10–5:30 💵 Free 🚇 Smithsonian, L'Enfant Plaza

🅢 National Archives

This William Pope-designed, neo-classical gem seems suitably grand to house the three cornerstone documents of American government: the Constitution, the Declaration of Independence and the Bill of Rights. These are in the building's rotunda, in specially designed helium-filled cases. With a mandate to preserve the government's history as reflected in its federal documents, the archives maintain hundreds of millions of pages of documents, as well as more than 100,000 reels of film and 200,000 sound recordings.

Here you can find the flight plan for *Apollo 11*, Abraham Lincoln's Emancipation Proclamation (which freed the nation's slaves on January 1, 1863), and the Marshall Plan (by which Europe was rebuilt after World War II).

🚼 195 E3 ✉ 7th Street and Pennsylvania Avenue N.W. ☎ 202/357-5000; www.archives.gov ⏰ Mid-Mar to Labour Day daily 10–7, Labor Day to mid-Mar 10–5:30 🚇 Archives/ Navy Memorial 💵 Free

🅖 International Spy Museum

If you love James Bond or are intrigued by the world of espionage, then you shouldn't pass up the fun and fascinating Spy Museum. It displays the world's largest collection of spy-related artifacts. The collection includes such gems as an original German Enigma coding machine, James Bond's Aston Martin DB-5 (complete with tire-shredders, drop-down machine guns and oil slick) from the movie *Goldfinger*, and lots of bugs, tiny cameras and other spy gadgets. Pick up tickets early in the day, this museum gets busy!

At the National Archives you can view the original Declaration of Independence, the Constitution and the Bill of Rights

The International Spy Museum is a popular venue with children and adults alike – enter the exciting world of espionage

🚻 195 D4 ✉ 800 F Street
☎ 202/393–7798 or 866/779-6873;
www.spymuseum.org 🕐 Apr–Aug daily
9–8; Sep–Mar 10–6. Hours can vary,
check the website 💷 Expensive
🚇 Gallery Place-Chinatown

Ford's Theatre

Built in 1861, Ford's Theatre is where President Abraham Lincoln was assassinated in 1865. That event so damaged the theater's business that it was forced to close, and it was eventually turned into offices. In the 1960s, however, the theater was renovated to look as it did the night Lincoln was shot. It still stages plays, and now also has a museum. When rehearsals are not taking place, hourly talks (daily 9:15– 4:15) describe the assassination. Visitors can tour the theater and see the presidential box where Lincoln sat on the fateful night. The basement

museum displays artifacts that include a piece of Lincoln's bloodstained coat and the actual murder weapon, a .44 derringer.
🚻 195 D4 ✉ 511 10th Street N.W. ☎ 202/347-4833;
www.fordstheatre.org 🕐 Daily 9–5 💷 Free 🚇 Metro Center or Federal Triangle

8 Smithsonian American Art Museum

The museum's collection traces the development of American art and includes excellent works by John Singer Sergeant and Winslow Homer, as well as over 400 works by artist George Caitlin who documented little-known Native American tribes in the 19th century. Modern pieces include works by Robert Motherwell, Willem de Kooning and others. The museum is housed in the renovated National Historic Landmark building with a curving double staircase and galleries illuminated by natural light.
🚻 195 E4 ✉ 8th and G streets N.W.
☎ 202/275-1500;
www.americanart.si.edu 🕐 Daily 11:30–7 💷 Free 🚇 Chinatown

9 National Portrait Gallery

The collection focuses on portraiture of or by Americans since the American Revolution. Among the many works is the "Lansdowne" portrait of George Washington by Gilbert

The Newseum's First Amendment Gallery explores the implications of the Bill of Rights

Stuart. Modern subjects include Marilyn Monroe and John Wayne.

➕ 195 E4 ✉ 8th and F streets N.W.
☎ 202/357-2700; www.npg.si.edu
🕐 Daily 11:30–7 ✋ Free
Ⓜ Chinatown

🔟 National Museum of the American Indian

Opened in late 2004, the museum is housed in a striking curved limestone building, surrounded by large rounded "Grandfather Stones" which evoke a natural environment. Inside, a wall of video screens offer visitors greeting in 150 native languages. The permanent displays focus on the peoples, spiritual world and contemporary life of native peoples throughout the western hemisphere. The presentations include multimedia and static exhibits that bring the world of Native Americans to life. Over 3,500 items on display include art, jewelry, religious pieces and everyday objects, from prehistoric to contemporary. Rotating exhibits show the works of the finest Native American artists.

➕ 195 E3 ✉ 4th Street and Independence Avenue S.W.
☎ 202/633-1000; www.nmai.si.edu 🕐 Daily 10–5:30 ✋ Free Ⓜ L'Enfant Plaza, Smithsonian

🔟 Newseum

Step behind the scenes and learn how the news is made and revisit five centuries of news history. Opened in fall 2007 with seven floors of galleries, theaters and visitor services, this fascinating museum is fun and entertaining as well as full of interesting hands-on exhibits, displays and up-to-the-second news delivered using the latest technology. The News History gallery presents 500 years of news history based on a collection of more than 30,000 historic newspapers. World news, with television news feeds from around the world, is available along with the daily front pages of 80 newspapers. Special galleries provide in-depth coverage of specific world events, including 9/11 and fall of the Berlin Wall.

➕ 195 E3 ✉ 555 Pennsylvania Ave., N.W. ☎ 888/639-7386; www.newseum.org 🕐 Daily 9–5 ✋ Expensive Ⓜ Archives

Where to...
Eat and Drink

Prices
Expect to pay per person for a meal, including drinks, tax and service
$ under $30 $$ $30–$60 $$$ over $60

RESTAURANTS

▼▼▼ Café Atlantico $$

This fashionable *nuevo-Latino* restaurant looks like it's been transported directly from Miami's South Beach, with three colorful floors, and patio dining in summer. Innovative cuisine under chef Katsuya Fukushima is matched by modern Latin artwork and background music. The menu changes regularly but always includes Caribbean, South American and Mexican dishes. Try the pre-theater tasting menu at dinner, or the multicourse *dim sum* weekend lunch menu. The South American wine list is great.

195 E4 ⊠ 405 8th Street at E Street N.W. 🕿 202/393-0812; www.cafeatlantico.com 🕒 Mon–Thu 11:30–2:30, 5–10, Fri 11:30–2:30, 5–11, Sat 11:30– 2:30, 5–11, Sun 11:30–2:30

▼▼▼ Ceiba $$

Ultra sleek and neutral tones set the stage for contemporary Latin American cuisine inspired by the culinary traditions of Veracruz in the Yucatan, São Paulo in Brazil, as well as Peru and Cuba. Latin-inspired desserts, boutique wines and a full-service bar round out the offerings.

194 C4 ⊠ 701 14th Street N.W. 🕿 202/393-3983, www.ceibarestaurant.com 🕒 Mon–Thu 11:30am–2:30pm, Fri 11:30–2:30, 5:30–11, Sat 5:30–11

▼▼▼▼ CityZen $$$

Enjoy world-class dining in the Mandarin Oriental Hotel's signature restaurant. Unique and very modern, the nouvelle-American cuisine is based on traditional dishes with original interpretations. Discover intriguing new flavors with specialties like panade-crusted sturgeon or grilled calotte of prime Midwestern beef.

195 D2 ⊠ 1330 Maryland Avenue S.W. 🕿 202/787-6868; www.mandarinoriental.com/hotel/5350 00039.asp 🕒 Tue–Thu 6–9:30pm; Fri–Sat 5:30–9:30pm

▼▼▼ D.C. Coast $$$

The high vault ceilings, large windows and pale wood furnishings, exude a California air. The bar buzzes with beautiful people and the city's financial elite. The cuisine includes a variety of seafood dishes. Try the grilled Scottish salmon, the double-cut pork chop or the Angus rib eye. The portions are generous and there's an extensive wine list.

194 C5 ⊠ 1401 K Street N.W. (in the Tower Building) 🕿 202/216-5988; www.dccoast.com 🕒 Mon–Fri 11:30–2:30 and 5:30–10.30, Sat 5:30–10.30

▼▼▼ Jaleo $$

Few places in town have more Spanish flavor than this casual restaurant that offers more than 50 hot and cold tapas, such as tiny lamb chops with rosemary, chorizo sausage with mashed potatoes, and stuffed mushrooms. Flamenco on Wednesday nights and a pre-theater menu.

195 E4 ⊠ 480 7th Street N.W. 🕿 202/628-7949; www.jaleo.com 🕒 Tue–Thu 11:30–11:30, Fri–Sat 11:30am–midnight, Sun–Mon 11:30–10

Les Halles $$

This old-style brasserie is one of the most exciting restaurants in town, with French waiters scurrying across the hardwood floors. The hanger steak with shallot sauce is recommended, and the steak tartare is prepared tableside. Other favorites include braised rabbit in a grainy mustard sauce and rotisserie leg of lamb. Personalities from the Hill are often found chatting by the bar.

195 D4 ⊠ 1201 Pennsylvania Avenue at 12th Street N.W.
202/347-6848; www.leshalles.net
Daily 11:30am–midnight

Marrakesh $$

Here, in a dining room decorated with Moroccan furnishings, carpets, oil lamps and hand-painted carvings, you have only one choice for dinner: a seven-course feast fit for kings. A three-salad platter may be followed by a pie layered with chicken, assorted nuts, eggs and almonds. Back-to-back entrées include chicken with lemon and olives and a selection of meats; couscous helps cleanse the palate. Fruits, mint tea and a Moroccan pastry follow. Belly dancing is performed during dinner. No credit cards.

195 E5 ⊠ 617 New York Avenue N.W. 202/393-9393; www.marrakesh.us Daily 6–11pm

Old Ebbitt Grill $$

The oldest and busiest saloon in Washington draws political insiders from the White House and nearby federal buildings as well as a large tourist crowd. Booths allow for uninterrupted conversation amid a splendid Victorian setting of early American paintings, antique gas chandeliers and a mahogany bar. In addition to an oyster bar, there's standard American cuisine, including seafood, steaks and homemade pasta. The Old Ebbitt also serves the city's most popular power breakfast.

194 C4 ⊠ 675 15th Street at F Street N.W. 202/347-4800; www.ebbitt.com Daily 7am–1am, Sat and Sun 8:30am–1am

Oceanaire Seafood Room $$

Stylish and busy, this restaurant has a daily menu with fresh seafood flown in from around the world. Seasonal favorites include salmon from the Copper River, Alaskan halibut and Dover sole. The portions are generous, and the dining room and oyster bar are both popular.

195 D4 ⊠ 1201 F Street N.W. 202/347-2277; www.theoceanaire.com Mon–Thu 11:30–10, Fri 11:30–11, Sat 5–11, Sun 5–9

701 Pennsylvania Avenue $$

Columns stretch to a high ceiling, candles flicker by night, and a piano and stand-up bass fill the dining room with music at 701. It has an international Wine Bar, and the state-of-the-art bar has dozens of vodkas. The modern Continental menu is light and innovative.

195 E3 ⊠ 701 Pennsylvania Avenue N.W. 202/393-0701; www.701restaurant.com Mon–Thu 11:30–3, 5:30–10:30, Fri 11:30–3, 5:30–11:30, Sat 5:30–11:30, Sun 5–9:30

Poste-Moderne Brasserie $$

Chic and modern, this bustling restaurant serves American cuisine. The seasonal menu has selections such as Virginia Kobe beef steak tartare with brioche, crispy skin wild striped bass with champ potatoes and red wine poached egg, and pumpkin ravioli. Housed in an old post office, the restaurant has high cast-iron ceilings, original skylights and plush booths.

195 E4 ⊠ 555 8th Street N.W. 202/783-6060; www.postebrasserie.com Mon–Fri 7–10, 11:30–2:30, 5–10 (also Fri 5–10:30), Sat 9–4, 5–10:30, Sun 9–4, 5–9

TenPenh $$$

TenPenh has topped expectations under chef Jeff Tunks of D.C. Coast

Where to...
Shop

The **Shops at National Place** (13th and F streets N.W.) are next to the National Press Building. Casual clothing shops and a few specialty stores are found in this small shopping center. **Macy's** (12th and G streets N.W.) is a complete department store offering the best brands.

For something more upscale, try the **Chanel Boutique** (1455 Pennsylvania N.W.) at the Willard Hotel. **Olsson's Books & Records** (418 7th Street N.W.) has a good selection of books, magazines and CDs.

Zenith Gallery (413 7th Street N.W.) is one of the city's most innovative art galleries.

The **Smithsonian Museum shops** offer fascinating gifts, crafts, books, jewelry and more.

(➤ 71). The dining room, filled with Asian antiques, serves Asian-American fusion cooking, ranging from halibut with Japanese bread-crumbs to raw oysters, lamb chops and fruit-filled spring rolls.

➕ **195 D4** ✉ **1001 Pennsylvania Avenue N.W.** ☎ **202/393-4500; www.tenpenh.com** 🕐 **Mon–Fri 11:30–2:30 and 5:30–10:30, Sat 5:30–11**

Zaytinya $

Enjoy a large selection of classic and contemporary Greek, Turkish and Lebanese *mezze*, small bites of food ideal for sharing. Selections are varied, including sea scallops with yogurt-dill sauce, vegetarian spanakopita, falafel and hummus, and desserts such as chocolate flan or cardamom *espuma* finished with espresso syrup. This popular restaurant is a great meeting spot with an upbeat clientele.

➕ **195 D4** ✉ **701 9th Street N.W.** ☎ **202/638-0800, www.zaytinya.com** 🕐 **Sun–Mon 11:30–10, Tue–Thu 11:30–11:30, Fri–Sat 11:30–midnight**

BARS

ESPN Zone

Three levels of sports: interactive games, 200 televisions, large video screen and special headphones, sports bar and restaurant.

➕ **195 D4** ✉ **555 12th Street N.W.** ☎ **202/783-3776** 🕐 **Sun–Thu 11:30–11, Fri 11:30am–midnight**

Fado Irish Pub

The young crowd enjoys live music every Wednesday and a good atmosphere on Saturday.

➕ **195 E4** ✉ **808 7th Street N.W.** ☎ **202/789-0066** 🕐 **Mon–Thu 11am–2am, Fri–Sat 11am–3am, Sun 11am–midnight**

Round Robin Bar

Enjoy cocktails in a sophisticated setting inside the Willard Inter-Continental Washington (➤ 41).

➕ **194 C4** ✉ **1401 Pennsylvania Avenue N.W.** ☎ **202/628-9100** 🕐 **Mon–Sat 11am–1am, Sun 11am–midnight**

Shelly's Backroom

The casual atmosphere contrasts with high-class martinis and ports, private humidors and big couches.

➕ **194 C4** ✉ **1331 F Street N.W.** ☎ **202/737-3003** 🕐 **Mon–Thu 11:30am–1:30am, Fri–Sat 11:30am–2:30am, Sun noon–1:30am**

The Tavern

Microbrews, cocktails, specialty beverages and light meals are on offer in a comfortable setting near the Convention Center.

➕ **195 D4** ✉ **999 9th Street N.W.** ☎ **202/898-9000, fax 202/289-0947**

CAFES

Teaism

The world's coffees and teas as well as gourmet snacks are served at this Asian-influenced café. A second branch is at 2009 R Street N.W.

➕ **197 F1** ✉ **800 Connecticut Avenue N.W.** ☎ **202/835-2233** 🕐 **Mon–Fri 7:30–5:30**

Where to...
Be Entertained

THEATER

Arena Stage

With an outstanding resident company, Arena – famed for having won the first Tony award outside New York – has three stages. Director Molly Smith has an eclectic taste in theater, but the performances are generally of a high standard.

✛ 195 E1 ⊠ 6th Street and Maine Avenue S.W. ☎ 202/488-3300

Ford's Theatre

Musicals and dramas are staged at the theater where Lincoln was shot (▶ 69). Dickens' *A Christmas Carol* plays annually, while the regular season covers a wide range.

✛ 195 D4 ⊠ 511 10th Street N.W. ☎ 202/347-4833

Shakespeare Theatre

The Shakespeare Theatre has one of the nation's top Shakespeare companies, which presents both Shakespearean and modern plays each season. Director Michael Kahn attracts high-caliber stars for his edgy productions, which are well-attended as well as well-acted. Every summer the theater presents two weeks of free "Shakespeare in the Park" at the Carter Barron Amphitheater (▶ 30).

✛ 195 E4 ⊠ 450 7th Street N.W. ☎ 202/547-1122

Warner Theatre

This distinguished venue sees a variety of performances, from dance pieces to concerts and comedy acts. The Broadway series and mainstream concerts are the general fare.

✛ 195 D4 ⊠ 13th and E streets N.W. ☎ 202/783-4000

DANCE

Dance Place

This innovative studio offers modern American and international dance performances.

✛ 200 off C5 ⊠ 3225 8th Street N.E. ☎ 202/269-1600

MUSIC

Verizon Center

Home of the Washington Wizards basketball team and Capitals hockey team, the Verizon Center is also the city's biggest concert facility. The complex houses all sorts of sports video games and virtual-reality machines as well, so visitors can play hockey with Wayne Gretzky or shoot hoops with Michael Jordan.

✛ 195 E4 ⊠ 601 F Street N.W. ☎ 202/628-3200

National Gallery of Art

Free classical music concerts on Sunday evenings in the West Garden Court from October to June at 6:30.

✛ 195 E3 ⊠ 6th Street and Constitution Avenue N.W. ☎ 202/842-6941

COMEDY AND CABARET

Capitol Steps

Washington's venerable political satire troupe, comprised of past Capitol Hill staffers, performs Friday and Saturday at 7:30pm at the Ronald Reagan Building and International Trade Center.

✛ 194 C4 ⊠ 1300 Pennsylvania Avenue N.W. ☎ 202/312-1555

Gross National Product

When in Washington, this hilarious group of political naysayers performs at the Warehouse Theater. "Son of a Bush" marked the beginning of the Bush administration.

✛ 195 E5 ⊠ 101 7th Street N.W. ☎ 202/783-7212

The West Mall

Getting Your Bearings

The west end of the National Mall, known as West Potomac Park, is where the capital's finest and most famous monuments are located. Rain or shine, this area is always busy as visitors wander along the broad sidewalks that crisscross the Mall from one monument to the next.

The West Mall is irregularly shaped, bounded by Constitution Avenue to the north, 14th Street to the west and south, and the Potomac River area to the east. In fine weather the crowds can be thick, as office workers and city dwellers join the throngs on the Mall to enjoy the fresh air and famous views of the monuments. But even on the busiest days, it always seems possible to find a less traveled walkway leading to a quiet corner of the Mall that you can call your own. It is also a delightful place to walk at night, when the paths and monuments are attractively lit. The monuments are open until midnight and the area is heavily policed.

    As it's easy to do a lot of walking here, wear comfortable shoes and in the summer have plenty of water with you. There are no restaurants at this end of the Mall, only numerous hot dog and hamburger refreshment stands at the memorials and along Constitution Avenue. For a better meal, walk half a mile north to the area around George Washington University and Foggy Bottom.

6
Arlingt
Nation
Cemete

ARLINGTO

**Preceding page:
Sunlight filters
through the
columns of the
Jefferson
Memorial**

**Left: The somber
statue of Lincoln
gazes out from
the Lincoln
Memorial**

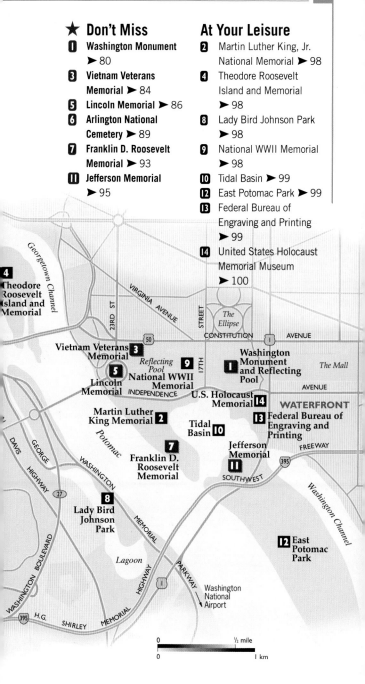

There's plenty to pack in to a day: the famous at rest, moving World War II memories and Washington's famous monuments.

The West Mall in a Day

8:00am

Plan to start the day with a lift...to the top of the 🔘 **Washington Monument** (below, ➤ 80–83). If you're in line for tickets promptly at 8am, the chances are good that you'll tour the monument before 9am (Ticket office opens Sep 1–Apr 15 at 9am.)

9:30am

Walk west from the Washington Monument to the Reflecting Pool and turn north to Constitution Gardens. Stroll across the wooden bridge to the island in the lake and pause to read some of the stones that are monuments to the original signers of the Declaration of Independence.

10:00am

Continue west to the 🔘 **Vietnam Veterans Memorial** (➤ 84–85). Walk slowly along the long black wall (it's okay to touch it) and look for mementos and flowers that others have left behind. Be sure to take in the two statues that stand at either end of the memorial (below, Frederick Hart's three soldiers).

10:30am

Walk a short way west to the 🔘 **Lincoln Memorial** (➤ 86–88). Climb up the front steps to experience the simple, majestic power of the Lincoln statue, and take time to read his simple, yet potent (and surprisingly short) Gettysburg Address. You'll also want to spend a few minutes on the front steps enjoying one of the classic views of the National Mall.

11:15am
Walk or take a cab (about a mile) across Arlington Memorial Bridge to **6 Arlington National Cemetery** (above, ► 89–92). Get a map at the visitor center and walk or ride the Tourmobile to see the highlights.

1:15pm
Take a cab or walk back across Arlington Memorial Bridge, south to Basin Drive and the Franklin D. Roosevelt Memorial. Vending trucks can provide a picnic lunch by the Tidal Basin.

1:45pm
Walk northeast along the Tidal Basin walkway to the **7 Franklin D. Roosevelt Memorial** (► 93–94). It only takes about an hour to stroll through the memorial, read the quotations and take in the museum.

2:45pm
Continue along the Tidal Basin walkway to the **11 Jefferson Memorial** (below, ► 95–97). Note the carved quotations on the walls and visit the small museum below the front portico (don't miss the excellent 12-minute video presentation).

3:45pm
There's still some time left in your day. You could walk around the **10 Tidal Basin** (► 99) to the docks and rent a paddleboat, or continue across to 14th Street to visit the **U.S. Holocaust Memorial Museum** (► 100).

8:30–9:30pm
The balmy evenings of summertime allow the extended pleasure of a late meander. After you've relaxed over a good evening meal at Kinkead's (► 102), return to the Mall for a stroll at dusk or just after dark to see the memorials lit by colored floodlights.

❶

Washington Monument

In 1833, Washington, D.C.'s National Monument Society announced its intention to erect a memorial to America's first president, George Washington (1732–99), "whose splendor will be without parallel in the world." Although it took more than 50 years for the group's plans to reach fruition, there are few who would deny that the Washington Monument is the city's most spectacular structure.

Access to the Washington Monument is from 15th Street. If you arrive early by car, you may find parking near the base of the monument, otherwise you have to circle the Mall looking for street parking. Timed entry tickets can be picked up from a 15th Street booth near the base of the monument. The earlier you arrive the better; in summer the tickets are usually gone by noon. Depending on when you arrive, your entry time will be anywhere from half an hour to five hours later.

When it was completed in 1885, the monument stood over 555 feet (169m) high and was the tallest structure in the world. Its record was usurped five years later by the 984-foot (300m), wrought-iron Eiffel Tower, but even today it remains the tallest masonry structure on the planet. Visible from virtually every part of the city, the monument acts like a magnet to visitors, and every year over 550,000 people wait patiently in line to take the one-minute elevator ride to the top, where the small summit room contains surprisingly small windows that nonetheless offer panoramic views of the city. Until recently hardier souls had the option of climbing the monument's 897 steps to the top, but this is now only possible on ranger-led tours. Beyond that there's not much to see and do here, but the monument's sheer physical size, its simple elegance and its status as an American icon make it a site to which every first-time Washington visitor should make a pilgrimage.

Perhaps no American is more deserving of a monument than George Washington, called the "Father of His Country." Born to a middle-class plantation farmer, he was a skilled outdoorsman and a trained surveyor. His fortunes improved dramatically when he married Martha Custis, a wealthy widow with impeccable social connections. His early military service was not distinguished, but he learned quickly from his mistakes. During the Revolutionary War he was given command of the colonies' Continental Army, and is credited with

When it was completed in 1885 the Washington Monument was the tallest structure in the world

Vital Statistics
- Total weight: 90,854 tons
- Total number of blocks: 36,491
- Cost: $1,187,710
- Type of exterior stones: white marble mostly from Baltimore, Maryland; some from Sheffield, Massachusetts
- Designer: Robert Mills

taking a ragged group of undisciplined soldiers and turning them into a cohesive and disciplined fighting force. Under Washington's command, the Continental Army lost more battles than it won, but it won the battles that counted, culminating in the surrender of British general Charles Cornwallis at Yorktown in 1781.

Washington's seemingly impossible victory over the world's greatest military power gave him an almost godlike stature among the people and the army. When it came time for Congress to choose the first president for the fledgling country, George Washington was their unanimous choice. He was respected for his moral strength, impeccable honesty and his ability to meet each challenge with level-headed determination. Equally important, he was trusted up and down the country, both North and South.

Washington accepted the presidency with reservations (he wanted to return to his life as a gentleman farmer in Virginia). But he also had a solid vision of what needed to be done to build the new government. During his two terms as president he was a stabilizing influence in the country's turbulent early years, and he established many of the relationships between the branches of government that still exist today.

The idea of building a monument to George Washington had been suggested many times since the end of the Revolutionary War. Indeed, Pierre L'Enfant's original plan for the city called for a large equestrian statue of Washington to

Reflecting Pool

Extending 2,000 feet (610m) from the steps of the Lincoln Memorial toward the National WWII Monument, the Reflecting Pool is one of the city's most captivating design elements. On still nights, seen from the Lincoln Memorial steps, the entire length of the Washington Monument is perfectly reflected. By day, visitors come to sit on the pool's edge and enjoy the surrounding views of the Mall and monuments. Open daily 8am–midnight. Admission free.

The Washington Monument and the Lincoln Memorial

The small windows at the top of the monument offer a view that has wowed visitors since 1885

be located in the center of the Mall, but no funds were available. In 1804, President Thomas Jefferson placed a modest stone commemorating Washington, where he hoped a larger monument would one day stand. That stone can still be seen a few paces from the base of the monument.

In 1832, Congress commissioned a marble statue of Washington for the Capitol Rotunda. The result – a classical, seated Washington, naked from the waist up and draped in robes – was so ridiculed that it was quickly removed. Today it can be seen in the National Museum of American History (► 62–64).

In 1833, architect Robert Mills unveiled an elaborate plan for a massive monument that included a huge, round building 100 feet high, surrounded by statuary and topped with a 500-foot (152.5m) stone obelisk. The Monument Society was forced to look at its financial resources and eventually opted for the stone obelisk alone.

Construction of the monument began in 1848, but by 1854, with it measuring 152 feet (46m), funds ran out. The structure was quickly roofed over and the project stopped. It wasn't until 1878 that work was resumed. By then the original supply of Maryland marble had been exhausted, and marble from Massachusetts had to be substituted to finish the monument in 1885. This created the slight color change that you can see a third of the way up. (Some park rangers will jokingly tell you it's the high water mark for the Potomac River.)

TAKING A BREAK

City planners have kept restaurants at a distance from the monuments of the West Mall. It's easy to find a lunch truck parked by the side of the street, but the offerings are minimal. The best option is **Red Sage** for Tex-Mex specialties.

🚇 194 C3 ✉ 15th Street, in the center of the Mall ☎ 202/426-6841; www.nps.gov/wash/ 🕐 Daily 9–4:45; closed July 4 💲 Free Ⓜ Smithsonian

3

Vietnam Veterans Memorial

Powerful, evocative and haunting, the Vietnam Veterans Memorial is Washington's first truly interactive memorial. When you first approach, the memorial's human scale and structural simplicity do little to prepare you for its emotional impact. But walk along the gleaming black walls etched with seemingly endless rows of names of the 58,226 soldiers killed or reported missing in action in Vietnam, and it delivers a potent message for all ages about the wound that is war.

The memorial is the brainchild of Vietnam veteran **Jan Scruggs**. Scruggs was wounded in Vietnam but survived his tour of duty, although many of his friends did not.

He envisioned a memorial in Washington, paid for by public donations "that would help heal a nation divided by this conflict." At the time, Vietnam was a war that many wanted to forget.

A visitor makes a rubbing of one of the names

Ridiculed by the press and the butt of many jokes, Scruggs' fledgling organization made national news when it was learned that they had only raised $114.50. But as the jokes made their rounds, more and more people heard of his goals. Slowly at first, and then faster, donations began pouring in. By 1980, the Vietnam Veterans Memorial Foundation had raised almost $9 million.

The memorial was designed by 21-year-old student **Maya Ling Yin**, whose plan was chosen from more than 1,000 entries in a national competition. Standing at the site, she said she "envisioned a wound in the earth." Her resulting design is an exercise in the dramatic power of understatement, consisting of two walls of black granite, each nearly 250 feet (75m) long, that meet, appropriately, in a broad V.

The entire structure lies below ground level. Each wall begins at just a few inches high and gently descends to where the walls join, at

Vital Statistics
- Designer: Maya Ling Yin
- Dedication: November 13, 1982
- Cost: $4,284,000
- Material: black granite from Bangalore, India
- Total length: 493 feet 6 inches (150.5m)

Above: The wall of names of those who gave their lives during the Vietnam War makes a simple but powerful statement

Inset: The memorial's designer, Maya Ling Yin

which point they are over 10 feet (3m) tall. The monument is made of black granite imported from India, and the entire length of its angled surface is etched with uniform letters spelling out the names of the dead and missing. (Those who are known dead are marked with a diamond; 11,000 names of soldiers missing in action are marked with a cross.) No mention is made of rank or status, leaving only the sense of a lost human life.

Eventually, traditionalists lobbied the government to add two statues with more conventional themes. At the west end of the site, a **sculpture of three soldiers** created by Frederick Hart captures the fear and uncertainty of the Vietnam War. At the eastern entrance, a **large bronze** by Glenna Goodacre serves as a tribute to the 11,000 women who served in Vietnam.

TAKING A BREAK

An alternative to the lunch trucks is to walk or cab to the Asian- inspired light American cuisine of the courtyard **Garden Café** in the State Plaza Hotel on F Street between 21st and 22nd.

🚑 194 A3 ✉ Bacon Drive and Constitution Avenue ☎ 202/634-1568; www.nps.gov/vive/ 🕐 Daily 8am–11:45pm 🎟 Free Ⓜ Smithsonian/Foggy Bottom

---

VIETNAM VETERANS MEMORIAL: INSIDE INFO

Top tip Every year, thousands of **offerings** are left along the wall: flowers, medals, cigarettes and even toys. This memorabilia is gathered up by staff and a small portion of the collection is on display at the Smithsonian until completion of the new Vietnam Veterans Memorial Center.

5

Lincoln Memorial

Ask a hundred Washington visitors which memorial they remember best, and chances are most will say the Lincoln Memorial. Rising gracefully above the west end of the National Mall, the building's clean, elegant lines are visible from almost every part of central Washington.

What gives the Lincoln Memorial such power is that its message exceeds the sum of its physical parts. More than a monument to one of America's greatest and most beloved presidents, Abraham Lincoln (1809–65), it is a memorial to the country's highest ideals of democracy and a reminder of the price the nation paid for unity. Even Washingtonians, jaded by daily political wranglings, have been known to take the rejuvenating walk up the granite steps to look into the eyes of "The Great Emancipator."

Walk up the steps and at the top turn around to enjoy the **view** of the Washington Monument and the Reflecting Pool, then enter the monument, where you will be met by the awesome 20-foot high (6m) **marble statue** of a seated Lincoln, by Daniel Chester French. Inside, on the north wall, you can read part of the text from Lincoln's second inauguration speech, in which he cites the need to "bind the nation's wounds."

Carved into the south wall is the text from his famous **Gettysburg Address**, delivered on November 19, 1863 and considered by many to be one of the most powerful speeches in American history.

Ironically, Lincoln was lambasted by the *Chicago Times* for the brevity of the speech, and Lincoln himself felt that the speech had been a failure. But its text – which begins "Four score and seven years ago, our forefathers brought forth on this continent a new nation, conceived in liberty, and dedicated to

The seated statue of Lincoln is considered one of sculptor Daniel Chester French's greatest works

the proposition that all men are created equal" – has left an indelible imprint.

Lincoln is best remembered as the man who, as 16th president, guided a bitterly divided America through the Civil War, a conflict that often saw family members fighting on opposing sides, and that nearly destroyed the young nation. He is also remembered as the architect of the Emancipation Proclamation, which freed the slaves and marked the beginning of the long and arduous struggle of African-Americans for civil rights.

Although many plans for a memorial to Lincoln had been proposed since the 1870s (suggestions included a huge pyramid and a highway from Washington to Gettysburg), it wasn't until architect Henry Bacon proposed a simple Greek temple in 1901 that the Senate gave its approval. Its dignified, solemn lines are in perfect harmony with its surroundings. The 36 Doric columns represent the 36 states that existed at the time of Lincoln's death. Above them are pictorial plates that represent the 48 states at the time the memorial was built.

As a symbol of freedom and democracy, the memorial has become a popular icon of the civil rights movement. The deep

irony of the nation's failure to achieve equality was felt at the memorial's 1922 dedication, when the African-American keynote speaker, Dr. Robert Moton, was not allowed to sit among the white speakers (who included President Warren Harding and Lincoln's son Robert) because of segregation laws.

In 1939, the monument's first starring role in a civil rights protest came about when soprano Marian Anderson – prevented from singing at Constitution Hall by the Daughters of the American Revolution (DAR) because of her color – gave a free concert to 75,000 listeners from its steps.

In 1963, Martin Luther King, Jr. chose the steps of the Lincoln Memorial as the stage from which he delivered to a crowd of 250,000 his famous speech "I Have a Dream."

The sculpted panels around the top of the monument represent the 48 states that existed when the memorial was built

TAKING A BREAK

The area lacks restaurants, but the National Park service operates a food kiosk that offers basic food (hotdogs and hamburgers), however the enjoyment of eating by the **Reflecting Pool** (► 82) can help make up for it.

➕ 194 A3 ✉ 23rd Street at the west end of the National Mall N.W.
☎ 202/426-6841; www.nps.gov/linc/ 🕐 Daily 24 hours; ranger available
9:30am–11:30pm 🎟 Free 🚇 Smithsonian/ Foggy Bottom

LINCOLN MEMORIAL: INSIDE INFO

Top tip See the memorial at least once when it is **lit up**. The best time is at dusk, or just after sunset.

Hidden gem If you want to learn more about Lincoln, try visiting the **American Presidency Exhibit** at the National Museum of American History (► 64).

6

Arlington National Cemetery

Arlington National Cemetery, like the pages of American history, is full of presidents and political figures, explorers, famous writers, musicians and poets. The acres of immaculately tended green lawns, with their endless rows of white headstones representing a quarter of a million men and women who have died in the service of their country, is very moving. Although the cemetery stands as a memorial to them, it is by no means a sorrowful place. The parklike grounds, elegant monuments, rolling lawns and stately trees create a sense of tranquility that offers a peaceful counterpoint to the urban bustle just across the Potomac.

Arlington Cemetery's headstones represent 250,000 American men and women who died for their country

The cemetery can be a very busy place, especially in good weather, when tour buses disgorge hundreds of visitors who make a pilgrimage to the grave of John F. Kennedy and the Tomb of the Unknowns. Over 4 million visitors come to the cemetery each year to see these sites and other popular attractions, including the Challenger Memorial and Arlington House, the historic home of General Robert E. Lee.

Unless you are visiting a family grave, you must park at the visitor center at the cemetery entrance and continue on foot or take the **Tourmobile**, which plays a taped commentary about

the attractions and travels through the cemetery every few minutes, allowing you to get on and off as you please. Tickets can be bought at a booth inside the visitor center.

As you enter the cemetery, to your right is the grave of **William Howard Taft** (1857–1930), the only president other than Kennedy to be buried here. Taft was not a brilliant president, but several years after his presidency he had a much more satisfying career as Chief Justice of the Supreme Court.

The Eternal Flame burns at the graveside of assassinated president John F. Kennedy

From Taft's graveside, you can walk up the hill to the marble terrace that holds the Eternal Flame and the grave of the 35th president, **John F. Kennedy**, who was assassinated in 1963.

Also buried here is his wife, **Jacqueline Kennedy Onassis**, and two of their children who died as infants (John Kennedy, Jr. is not buried here). The grave site itself is simple and elegant. Inscribed here are several of JFK's best-known quotes.

A few steps away, a plain white cross marks the grave of his brother **Robert F. Kennedy**, who was assassinated during the presidential primaries in 1968.

From the Kennedy grave, a path leads uphill to **Arlington House**, which was originally built as a memorial to George Washington by his adoptive son, George Washington Custis. The house was passed to his daughter Mary and her dashing military husband, Robert E. Lee. In 1861, as the Civil War loomed close, President Lincoln offered Lee the command of the Union Army. But Lee could not bring himself to lead an invasion of his beloved Virginia, and instead chose to

Vital Statistics
- Acres: 612 (248ha)
- Number of graves: 300,000
- Dedicated: June 15, 1864
- Funerals held annually: 7,000
- Number of freed slaves interred: over 3,800
- Number of astronauts: 16
- Number of U.S. Supreme Court justices: 12
- Number of U.S. presidents: 2

The Tomb of the Unknowns:
- Weight: 79 tons
- Cost: $48,000
- Opened to the public: April 9, 1932

Famous People at Arlington National Cemetery

- Audie Murphy: the most decorated soldier of World War II and star of over 40 movies
- Glenn Miller (left): famed band leader, died in a military plane crash in 1944
- Robert Edwin Peary and Admiral Richard E. Byrd: Arctic explorers
- Mary Robert Rhinehart: novelist and first female war correspondent (WWI)
- Dashiell Hammett: mystery novelist, author of *The Maltese Falcon*

resign his Union commission and leave Arlington House to take command of the Confederate Army.

The Union Army took control of the original 1,100-acre (405ha) site as a military encampment and Mary Lee was forced to flee, taking only a few valuables with her. In 1864, the government appropriated the property to be used as a national cemetery. Although Robert E. Lee eventually returned to Virginia, he never petitioned the government for the return of his property, feeling it might reopen the nation's recent wounds.

The National Park Service restored the house and opened it in 1972 as the **Robert E. Lee Memorial**. The rooms have been furnished as they were when Lee lived here. Of particular interest is the parlor, where the Lees were married in 1831, and Lee's study, where he wrote his resignation letter to Lincoln. The most arresting feature of the house is its panoramic view of Washington, D.C. In front of the house is the grave of Pierre

e Changing
the Guard
remony at
e Tomb of
e Unknowns,
ich is
arded 24
urs a day

L'Enfant, the man who designed the capital city.

From Arlington House, it is about a 0.3-mile (0.5km) stroll to the **Tomb of the Unknowns**, which is guarded 24 hours a day by soldiers from the Third U.S. Infantry (the Old Guard).

The elaborate **Changing of the Guard** ceremony takes place every half-hour in summer and every hour in winter, and is one of the cemetery's highlights. The tomb itself contains four sarcophagi. One holds the remains of an unknown World War I soldier, one a World War II soldier, and a third holds remains from the Korean War. The fourth is empty. It originally held the remains of an unknown Vietnam War soldier, but DNA testing made it possible to identify the remains, and offers the hope that there may never again be another unknown soldier.

The USS *Mai...* Memorial commemorat... the 1898 sinking of the U.S. warship in Havana Harbor

Two other memorials are a short walk away. The **Challenger Memorial** honors the seven ill-fated astronauts who died when the space shuttle *Challenger* exploded on launch. Nearby, the mast of the **USS Maine** marks a memorial dedicated to the sailors who died when the *Maine* was mysteriously sunk in Havana Harbor in 1898, triggering the Spanish-American War.

TAKING A BREAK

There are no restaurants in or near the cemetery, but try out the reasonable prices and huge helpings of chicken and prime rib at **Tom Sarris' Orleans House**, one stop north on the Metro (1213 Wilson Boulevard, Rosslynn, open Mon–Fri 11–10, Sat–Sun 4–10).

✚ 198 C3　✉ At the west end of Arlington Memorial Bridge　☎ 703/607-8000; www.arlingtoncemetery.org　🕐 Apr–Sep 8–7; Oct–Mar daily 8–5　💷 Free; Tourmobile inexpensive　Ⓜ Arlington Cemetery

7

Franklin D. Roosevelt Memorial

Faced with the inevitability of being honored by a monument, Franklin Delano Roosevelt (1882–1945) was adamant that "it should be no larger than my desk." Fortunately his wish was ignored. Beside the edge of the Tidal Basin and surrounded by Japanese cherry trees, the Roosevelt Memorial is one of the most enjoyable of Washington's monuments.

President Franklin Delano Roosevelt led the United States through some of the darkest years of the 20th century

Consisting of four outdoor "rooms," the memorial blends sculpture, walkways, waterfalls and garden spaces into an inviting whole that Roosevelt himself would have found delightful.

As America's 32nd president, FDR led the country through 12 of the most turbulent years in the 20th century, including both the Great Depression and World War II. Each of the memorial's semienclosed spaces is dedicated to one of Roosevelt's four terms in office (he died shortly after his fourth inauguration in 1945).

The first two rooms cover the **Great Depression** and his **New Deal**. Here, a sculpture depicts the unemployed waiting in bread lines, while a mural opposite shows people enthusiastically

Each outdoor "room" in the memorial represents a different period of Roosevelt's presidency – these sculptures depict the Great Depression

working on government-created "New Deal" projects, such as building bridges, roads and schools, and creating art and music.

The next two rooms cover the **war years**. Roosevelt was often portrayed as a somber father figure leading the nation with firm resolve through Word War II. Here, the broken stones and tumbling waterfall – intended to convey turmoil – instead create a restful atmosphere. Here, too, is a bronze sculpture of Roosevelt's wife, Eleanor, whose strength and resolve were a key to his success.

Missing from the monument until recently was a depiction of FDR in a wheelchair. A victim of polio at age 39, Roosevelt required a wheelchair except when he stood for a speech. He avoided being seen in one, however, and only allowed the press to film him from the waist up. The original monument depicts a seated FDR whose cape conceals his wheelchair. Under pressure from disability groups, however, on January 1, 2001 a second bronze was placed near the entrance showing FDR in a wheelchair he built himself out of a kitchen chair and bicycle parts.

Below: The famous cherry trees by the Tidal Basin

Below right: Thomas Jefferson was the third president and wrote the Declaration of Independence

TAKING A BREAK

There are no food services at the memorial. In good weather, however, **lunch trucks** park in profusion all around.

✚ 194 B2 ✉ West Basin Drive, on the west side of the Tidal Basin ☎ 202/426-6841; www.nps.gov/frde/ 🕐 Daily 24 hours; ranger available 9:30am–11:30pm 💵 Free 🚇 Smithsonian

FRANKLIN D. ROOSEVELT MEMORIAL: INSIDE INFO

Top tips Visit late March or early April when the **cherry blossoms** are at their peak.
• The memorial's **small museum** does a good job of relating the details of Roosevelt's presidency.

Jefferson Memorial

Diplomat, scientist, gifted writer, farmer, lawyer, botanist, architect, mathematician and orator, Thomas Jefferson (1743–1826) was every inch the Renaissance man. He also served as the third president of the United States, from 1802 to 1809. In 1926, architect John Russell Pope set out to create a memorial honoring the multidimensional Jefferson. The resulting elegant structure is a symphony of neoclassical style, with graceful columns and a rounded dome, mirroring the architectural style Jefferson himself loved. Many people believe it is Pope's greatest creation and ranks as one of the most beautiful memorials in Washington.

Faint Praise

At a gathering of Nobel Peace Prize winners, President John F. Kennedy quipped: "You are the greatest assembly of talent in the White House since Thomas Jefferson dined here alone."

The entrance to the Jefferson Memorial faces north, looking across the Tidal Basin to the Washington Monument, and beyond to the White House. Inside the memorial, the gently curved rotunda surrounds a 19-foot high (5.5m) **bronze statue**, sculpted by Rudolph Evans, of a standing Jefferson, looking distinguished as an elder statesman. Above the statue is inscribed a Jefferson quote: "I have sworn upon the altar of God eternal hostility against every form of tyranny over the mind of man."

Words were perhaps Jefferson's finest tools, and several other quotes appear here, including his

famous, often-quoted lines from the Declaration of Independence: "We hold these truths to be self-evident: that all men are created equal, that they are endowed by the creator with certain inalienable rights, that among these are life, liberty, and the pursuit of happiness… ."

The monument nestles graciously into its surroundings at the south end of the Tidal Basin amid 2.5 acres (1ha) of landscaping originally designed by Frederick Law Olmsted, who designed New York's Central Park. A small, well-planned museum and a gift shop lie below ground level under the memorial's front portico.

The **museum**'s numerous displays on Jefferson include a brief but effective video that highlights his wide-ranging talents and contributions to the country.

Outside, a broad **walkway** leads around the Tidal Basin, providing an inviting place to stroll, particularly to the nearby Franklin D. Roosevelt Memorial (► 93–94).

Begun in 1938, the Jefferson Memorial – conceived as one site in the five-point plan for central Washington – did not get off to a smooth start. Some residents were appalled at the number of beautiful Japanese cherry trees that had to be uprooted to make way for it, and protesters chained themselves to the trees to delay construction. In addition, the building's 32,000 tons of marble and limestone proved too heavy for the soft soil around the Potomac, so a massive foundation had to be built of concrete pillars that extend almost 140 feet (43m) down to bedrock. It was dedicated on April 13, 1943, the 200th anniversary of Jefferson's birth.

Above: The view from Jefferson Memorial takes in the Washington Monument and the Tidal Basin

Right: Incorporating classical architectural styles that Jefferson himself favored, the memorial has been called one of Washington's most beautiful buildings

JEFFERSON MEMORIAL: INSIDE INFO

Top tips Many say the memorial is at its most beautiful **just after dark**, when it is dramatically lit from inside.
- The best time of year to visit is in **late March or early April**, when the hundreds of cherry trees surrounding the memorial and Tidal Basin are in blossom.

TAKING A BREAK

There is a small **snack stand** at the entrance to the parking area. Other than that, as elsewhere at this end of the Mall, your best bet is picking up a hot dog at any of the ubiquitous roadside catering trucks parked along the street. Take it to the Tidal Basin, pick out a park bench and dine with a view.

✚ 194 C1 ✉ West Basin Drive S.W. ☎ 202/426-6841; www.nps.gov/thje/ ⏰ Daily 24 hours; ranger available 9:30am–11:30pm 🎟 Free 🍴 Snack stand: $ Ⓜ Smithsonian, L'Enfant Plaza

At Your Leisure

2 Martin Luther King, Jr. National Memorial

This powerful yet serene memorial at the edge of the Tidal Basin, opening in 2008, honors Martin Luther King, Jr. A crescent-shaped stone wall bears excerpts from his speeches, and a 30-foot (9m) centerpiece, the Stone of Hope, depicts a likeness of Dr. King. Flowing water elements, landscaped areas, and niches for quiet reflection, support the "from despair to hope" theme of the memorial.

🔢 194 B2 ✉ On the Tidal Basin adjacent to the Franklin D. Roosevelt Memorial ☎ (888) 484-3373, www.mlkmemorial.org 🕐 Daily, dawn to dusk 🖐 Free 🚇 Smithsonian

4 Theodore Roosevelt Island and Memorial

One of America's most beloved presidents, Theodore "Teddy" Roosevelt also was an avid conservationist. Appropriately, his memorial is both simple and surrounded by nature. Theodore Roosevelt Island lies in the Potomac River directly across from the John F. Kennedy Center. Access to the island is from the Arlington side via a small footbridge from Lady Bird Johnson Park.

The island covers 88.5 acres (36ha) with 2.5 miles (4km) of trails that wind through the woodlands.

Occasional wildlife can be seen, including ducks and Canada geese. In the center of the island, the plazalike memorial has a 17-foot (5m) bronze statue of President Roosevelt in a classic speaking pose, with his fists raised and his face animated.

🔢 198 C5 ✉ Parking lot is off George Washington Memorial Parkway, just past Theodore Roosevelt Memorial Bridge ☎ (703) 289-2500; www.nps.gov/this/ 🕐 Daily dawn–dusk 🖐 Free 🚇 Rosslyn

Right: A spring day by the Potomac at Lady Bird Johnson Park

8 Lady Bird Johnson Park

This popular park lies along the strip of land between Arlington National Cemetery and the Potomac. In springtime the meadows here are carpeted in wildflowers planted as a tribute to Lady Bird Johnson, America's first lady from 1963 to 1969. At the south end of the park, trails lead through a stand of white pine and dogwood trees that commemorate President Lyndon B. Johnson (1908–73).

🔢 199 E2 ✉ Between Arlington National Cemetery and the Potomac River ☎ www.nps.gov/lyba/ 🕐 Daily dawn–dusk 🖐 Free 🚇 Arlington Cemetery, Pentagon

9 National WWII Memorial

This simple yet moving monument honors the 16 million men and women who served in the U.S. armed forces, the 40,000 who died, and those who served at home during World War II. The two large granite pavilions at each end of the open plaza represent the Atlantic and Pacific theaters of war and the 56 smaller pillars represent the states and territories that provided troops

to the war effort. The plaza's open airy design and lively fountains have made a popular mid-mall gathering place for families and it is far from a somber place. World War II veterans can sometimes be found at the memorial and are usually open to talking about their experiences.

✚ 199 F4 ✉ Mid-mall on 17th Street between the Washington Monument and the Lincoln Memorial
☎ National Park Service: 202/426-6841; www.nps.gov/nwwm ⏰ Daily
🎟 Free Ⓜ Smithsonian

🔟 Tidal Basin

Spanning most of the distance between the Jefferson and Lincoln memorials, the Tidal Basin is where you can meander and take in views of the monuments. A broad sidewalk follows the water's edge, and well-placed benches offer an inviting place to stop and rest your feet. Once a marshy inlet of the Potomac, the basin today is part of the city's flood-control system. A walk around the Tidal Basin is well rewarded in the evening, when the memorials are attractively lit, and in early April, when cascades of pink and white cherry blossoms cover the landscape. There's also a boathouse where you can rent paddleboats by the hour.

✚ 194 B2 ✉ Southeast of the Lincoln Memorial between Independence Avenue and 14th Street ⏰ Daily dawn–midnight 🎟 Free
Ⓜ Smithsonian, L'Enfant

🔟 East Potomac Park

If you have time to enjoy jogging and long walks by the river, this is the place to come. The park extends from the Tidal Basin along a peninsula to Hains Point, and the north end is home to some of the 3,000 cherry trees planted around the Tidal Basin. The park's 3-mile (5km) loop road is closed to traffic on weekends, making it a

The unique sculpture *The Awakening* rises from the ground at Hains Point

haven for cyclists and roller bladers. There is a public golf course and a swimming pool, which you are welcome to use. At Hains Point, you can marvel at *The Awakening*, a sculpture that depicts a buried giant rising out of the earth.

✚ 194 C1 ✉ Along Ohio Drive, south of the Tidal Basin ⏰ Daily dawn–midnight 🎟 Free
Ⓜ Smithsonian, L'Enfant Plaza

🔟 Federal Bureau of Engraving and Printing

There's something mesmerizing about watching an endless stream of dollars coming off the press, and that

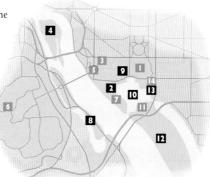

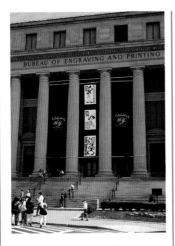

At the Federal Bureau of Printing and Engraving you can watch millions of dollars being printed

is the primary draw at the Federal Bureau of Printing and Engraving. This is where most of the nation's money is printed (there is a second printing plant in Fort Worth, Texas). Almost half a billion dollars' worth of currency is printed here every day, most of it going to replace worn bills taken out of circulation.

The bureau offers a 20-minute tour of its facility, during which visitors are led along narrow hallways where they can look through into the rooms where the cash is printed. The tour is popular, and it's a good idea to get your tickets (available at the door) in advance, as most days they are sold out by noon.

⊞ 194 C2 ⊠ 14th and C streets S.W. ☎ 202/874-2330; www.moneyfactory.com ⏰ Mon–Fri tours every 15 min from 9am–10:45am and 12:30pm–2pm. Ticket booth opens at 8am for same-day tickets; call first as tours may be canceled 🎟 Free 🚇 Smithsonian, L'Enfant Plaza

14 United States Holocaust Memorial Museum

Powerful, disturbing and unforgettable, the United States Holocaust Memorial comprises four floors filled with photographs, personal artifacts and multimedia exhibits that relate the story of the systematic extermination of millions of people by the Nazis during World War II.

The museum's exhibits are divided into three separate time frames. The first covers life in Germany before the Nazis in the 1930s. The second relates the Nazis' rise to power and their campaign of genocide, and the third section describes the liberation by the Allies and the period of turmoil that followed. Due to their content, the main exhibits are not recommended for children under the age of 11; but there is a special children's exhibit that follows the story of Daniel, a young boy who was sent to the concentration camps.

This is a popular museum, and timed passes (which are available at the main desk and often sold out by midmorning) are required for entry into the main exhibit. You can get advance tickets (fee charged) from tickets.com at 800/400-9373.

⊞ 194 C2 ⊠ 100 Raul Wallenberg Place near the corner of 14th Street and Independence Avenue ☎ 202/488-0400; www.ushmm.org ⏰ Daily 10–5:30 (pass desk closes 4pm); café 8:30–4:30; closed Yom Kippur 🍴 Café: $$ 🎟 Free 🚇 Smithsonian/L'Enfant Plaza

Where to...
Eat and Drink

Prices

Expect to pay per person for a meal, including drinks, tax and service
$ under $30 $$ $30–$60 $$$ over $60

RESTAURANTS

☞☞ Aditi $

This small, unassuming restaurant consistently wins praise for its excellent cuisine and is one of the most authentic Indian restaurants in Washington. Order a tandoori platter, sample the vegetarian or seafood curries, try one of the lamb or beef specialties, or go for a rice dish. Whatever you order, you'll need some delicious Indian bread to accompany your meal. Simply decorated with lavender walls and Indian artwork, Aditi's upper floor offers more space if the downstairs gets too crowded.

🚹 196 B2   🖃 3299 M Street near 33rd Street N.W.   ☎ 202/625-6825
🕐 Mon–Thu 11:30–2:30, 5:30–10, Fri–Sat 11:30–10:30, Sun noon–2:30, 5:30–10

☞☞☞ The Bombay Club $$

The subtle interior of this classic British Colonial dining room is punctuated with pictures of British rulers and the Maharajah. In addition to the service, which is friendly, attentive and never hurried, the food at Bombay Club is outstanding. Tandoori dishes and curries, as well as an exquisite selection of seafood and vegetarian plates, make up the menu. Don't forget an order of *nan* – a delicious refined-flour flat bread sprinkled with onion seeds – to calm the palate.

🚹 194 B4   🖃 815 Connecticut Avenue at H Street N.W.   ☎ 202/659-5012; www.bombayclubdc.com
🕐 Mon–Fri 11:30–2:30, 5:30–10:30, Sat 5:30–11pm, Sun 11:30–2:30, 5:30–9

☞☞☞ Corduroy $$

Cozy and modern, one of Washington's finest restaurants is tucked away on the second floor of the Four Points Sheraton Hotel. Chef Tom Power offers the finest foods of the season, often fresh from nearby farms. The New American cuisine presents ingredients whose natural flavors are enhanced by a delightful execution. Entrees might include crispy striped bass with sherry vinegar sauce or Copper Ridge Farm prime beef rib eye with rutabaga gratin and mushroom sauce. Vegetarian plates, salads, fresh breads, a diverse wine list and superb desserts complete the menu.

🚹 195 D5   🖃 1201 K Street N.W.   ☎ 202/589-0699.
www.corduroydc.com   🕐 Mon–Fri noon–2:30, 5:30–10:30, Sat 5–11

☞☞☞ Equinox $$

Chef-owner Todd Gray is the most important reason to visit Equinox. One of Washington's most innovative chefs, Gray has created a modern American menu that will delight. Dishes are light, sophisticated and regionally based. Entrees include seared yellowfin tuna, grilled Argentine rib eye and medallions of venison. There's also a six-course tasting menu. Cooking classes are held on various Saturdays.

🚹 194 B5   🖃 818 Connecticut Avenue N.W.   ☎ 202/331-8118; www.equinoxrestaurant.com
🕐 Mon–Sat 11:30–2, 5:30–10 (also Fri–Sat 10–10:30), Sun 5–9

Galileo $$$

Considered one of the top Italian kitchens in America, Galileo is the flagship restaurant of esteemed chef-owner Roberto Donna and celebrates Italy's Piedmont region. The fixed-price five-course menu lets you sample the greatest variety of plates for the most reasonable price (an eight-course menu can also be sampled). While all the dishes are first-rate, the braised-beef ravioli in red wine sauce and the white-truffle risotto are excellent choices. Privileged diners may choose to sit in the chef's "Laboratorio del Galileo," where Donna himself cooks for up to 25 people three nights a week.

✛ 197 E1 ⊠ 1110 21st Street N.W. ☎ 202/293-7191; www. robertodonna.com Ⓖ Mon–Fri 11:30–10, Sat–Sun 5:30–10

I Ricchi $$$

Although not as well known as Galileo (above), this restaurant is a bit less expensive and equally recommended. With Tuscan cuisine, the chefs at I Ricchi focus on the quality of food over creative presentation. Hearty steaks and seafood skewers are cooked in the wood-burning oven, and the fresh soups, salads and pastas should not be neglected. Reserve ahead, as I Ricchi is always crowded.

✛ 197 F2 ⊠ 1220 19th Street N.W. ☎ 202/835-0459; www.iricchi.com Ⓖ Mon–Fri 11:30–2 and 5:30–10:30, Sat 5:30–10:30

Kinkead's $$$

Chef-owner Bob Kinkead consistently wins praise for his American brasserie emphasizing local and national seafood. His modern multilevel restaurant, in one of D.C.'s oldest town homes, includes a handsome café and raw seafood bar downstairs, with more formal dining upstairs. The dinner menu changes daily, always including exquisite seafood such as *pepita*-crusted salmon or pepper-seared tuna with a *pinot noir* sauce. The wine list is excellent. Be sure to reserve ahead, as this is one of D.C.'s most frequented restaurants.

✛ 194 A4 ⊠ 2000 Pennsylvania Avenue at 20th Street N.W. ☎ 202/296-7700; www.kinkead.com Ⓖ Sun–Thu 11:30–10, Fri 11:30–10:30, Sat 5:30–10:30; daily raw bar 5:30–11

Marcel's $$$

Robert Wiedmaier is one of Washington's most celebrated chefs. He has now formed his own restaurant, named for his young son, Marcel. His beautiful dining room is country French in style, with stone walls, wrought-iron chandeliers and, gracing each table, sterling silver place settings. Wiedmaier spares little expense when he is selecting his products, driving to Pennsylvania to buy quail and pheasant, importing *foie gras* and seeking out the best venison on the market. The result is a truly memorable dining experience. Marcels offers complimentary valet parking and shuttle service to and from the John F. Kennedy Center.

✛ 197 D1 ⊠ 2401 Pennsylvania Avenue N.W. ☎ 202/296-1166; www.marcelsdc.com Ⓖ Mon–Thu 5:30–10, Fri–Sat 5:30–11, Sun 5:30–9:30

Miss Saigon $

An intimate dining room, sheltered by straw hats and small palm trees, is illuminated by tiny white lights. Miss Saigon attracts a mainly Georgetown-based crowd at lunch and a more diverse group at dinner, with attentive and relaxed service afternoon and night. Solo diners will feel comfortable here, and they can pick up a quick lunch during the week. An inexpensive menu allows mixing of dishes like caramel salmon, vegetarian spring rolls, crispy calamari and even seafood with noodles in an oyster sauce.

✛ 196 C2 ⊠ 3057 M Street at 31st Street N.W. ☎ 202/333-5545 Ⓖ Mon–Thu 11:30–10:30, Fri–Sat noon–11, Sun noon–10:30

The Oval Room $$

The dining room and trendy bar of this casually elegant establishment re-create the shape of the president's Oval Office and manage to lure the president's staff. In the main dining area, an enormous mural of past presidents, first ladies, foreign dignitaries and other celebrities creates a conversation piece. Choosing from the contemporary American menu can be tricky given the variety – consider the seafood soup or salad, followed by grilled rockfish with mushrooms, mussels and a spicy tomato sauce. Piano music is played Tuesday to Saturday, and a pre-theater menu is available from 5:30 to 6:45.

✚ 194 B4 ⊠ 800 Connecticut Avenue at H Street N.W. ☎ 202/463-8700; www.ovalroom.com
Ⓒ Mon–Thu 11:30–3, Fri 11:30–3, 5:30–10:30, Sat 5:30–10:30

The Prime Rib $$$

Washington's best-known steak house has the air of a private executive club carried over from the 1920s. The formal art deco dining room is a striking display of comfortable booths with black leather and white linens, fresh flowers and soft candlelight. It is not uncommon to see senators and high-ranking government officials dining at these tables. Tuxedo-clad waiters deliver tender beef under the spell of piano and stand-up bass, while bartenders serve martinis and vodka tonics to the veritable who's who around the large black bar. Among the top steaks to appease the appetite are the signature prime rib, the New York strip and the filet mignon. Jacket required.

✚ 194 A5 ⊠ 2020 K Street between 20th and 21st streets N.W.
☎ 202/466-8811; www.theprimerib.com Ⓒ Mon–Thu 11:30–3, 5–11, Fri–Sat 5–11:30

Taberna del Alabardero $$

Bas-relief carvings and silk drapes adorn this beautiful restaurant's high ceiling, while subdued lighting, original Spanish paintings and quiet music create an elegant setting. The Taberna offers a rich selection of hot and cold tapas; among the best are the mushrooms in white wine, shrimp sautéed in olive oil and spicy Spanish chorizo (sausage). The dinner menu is extraordinarily varied – the paella Valenciana (shellfish on a bed of Spanish rice) is the best in the city. Ask the staff to match a Spanish wine with your meal.

✚ 194 B5 ⊠ 1776 I Street (entrance on 18th Street) N.W. ☎ 202/429-2200; www.alabardero.com Ⓒ Mon–Fri 11:30–2:30, 5:30–10:30, Sat 5:30–10:30

BARS

Brickskeller

No Washington pub surpasses Brickskeller for sheer beer variety. With over 1,000 brands from across the globe, it has something for even the most exacting beer lovers. In addition to the pub, there's a restaurant serving standard bar food and a hotel upstairs for late-night drinkers. A DJ rocks the house on Saturday nights.

✚ 197 E2 ⊠ 1523 22nd Street N.W. ☎ 202/293-1885 Ⓒ Mon–Fri 11:30am–2am, Sat–Sun 6pm–2am (also Fri–Sat 2–3am)

Buffalo Billiards

If you're looking for a wide open space in the heart of Dupont Circle, visit this vast basement pool hall with Western decor. It's a casual but lively place, the Tex-Mex food is above average, and the games – you can try out nine ball, table shuffleboard and darts – will make you feel like a kid again. Stop in the snooker table room and you can almost imagine that you're in a speakeasy straight out of a John Wayne film. During happy hour, you can smoke cigars and sip Guinness with the city's busiest and brightest.

✚ 197 F2 ⊠ 1330 19th Street N.W. ☎ 202/331-7665 Ⓒ Mon–Thu 4pm–2am, Fri 4pm–3am, Sat 11:30am–3am, Sun 11:30am–1am

Where to...
Shop

The West Mall area is better equipped for sightseeing (with all the major national monuments) and entertainment than for shopping, but here are a few ideas.

BOOKS

Better than most libraries, the vast **Borders Books & Music** (18th and L streets N.W.) has two floors of books, an extensive magazine selection and a music store. And, unlike at a library, you can stop in the café for a sandwich or a cappuccino.

CLOTHES AND SHOES

At **Britches of Georgetowne** (1776 K Street N.W.), there is an abundant supply of men's suits, shoes and buff weekend wear.

Ann Taylor (1611 Connecticut Avenue N.W.) and **Talbots** (1122 Connecticut Avenue N.W.) offer classic women's clothing.

Find shoes to match at nearby **Nine West** (1001 Connecticut Avenue N.W.).

Just across from the historic Mayflower Hotel, **Riziks** (1100 Connecticut Avenue N.W.), a very chic boutique with high-end suits and evening wear, stands next to the more casual Gap and the lycra-spandex Express.

Bedazzled (1507 Connecticut Avenue N.W.) the ultimate bead and craft shop sells ancient trade beads to contemporary glass beads.

The shops at **2000 Pennsylvania Avenue** N.W., located in Foggy Bottom, cater to the hip students of nearby George Washington University. You can stock up on jeans and the latest fashions at Gap or browse the newest techno CDs at Tower Records.

Where to...
Be Entertained

THEATER

Lisner Auditorium

The enormous theater at George Washington University hosts classical music, pop and dance.

🚇 194 A4 🖾 21st and H streets N.W. ☎ 202/994-6800; www.lisner.org

Screen on the Green

On Monday nights at sunset July through August, head for the National Mall to watch the city's answer to a drive-in. Classic films like "Casablanca" illuminate the Mall, and, thanks to a booming sound system, there's no such thing as a bad seat.

🚇 194 B3 🖾 Between 4th and 7th streets on the National Mall ☎ 877/262-5866

MUSIC

Corcoran Gallery of Art

Free classical jazz concerts on the first and third Wednesday of the month. Phone for details.

🚇 194 B4 🖾 500 17th Street at New York Avenue N.W. ☎ 202/639-1770

DAR Constitution Hall

Big-name concerts ranging from R&B to jazz and pop take place in this large auditorium.

🚇 194 B3 🖾 18th and C streets N.W. ☎ 202/628-4780

Farragut Square

Free concerts are held at noon on summer Thursdays in this park.

🚇 194 B5 🖾 17th and K streets N.W. ☎ 202/619-7222

The White House and the North

Getting Your Bearings

Elegant architecture, early history, superb art galleries and a world-class zoo are the high points of Northwest Washington. Of course, the most famous residence here is the White House, but there also are the historic and architecturally splendid houses of Embassy Row, Dupont Circle and Adams-Morgan, as well as the beautifully restored 18th-century row houses of Georgetown. Close to the White House, some of Washington's most opulent buildings contain public attractions such as the Octagon Museum, the renowned Corcoran Gallery of Art and the Renwick Gallery.

The lively, and sometimes pretentious, neighborhood of Georgetown in Northwest D.C. blends elegance and funk, as the nouveau riche and politically connected rub elbows with students from Georgetown and George Washington universities. Georgetown is a hotbed of great shopping opportunities and restaurants, and some of the area's best ethnic dining can be found in the nearby Dupont Circle and Adams-Morgan neighborhoods. Farther north, the lushly wooded ravine of Rock Creek Park is home to several historic attractions, including the charming Peirce Mill. Here you'll also find the world-renowned National Zoological Park, whose two favorite residents, giant pandas Tian Tian and Mei Xiang, have become major celebrities.

In the 1800s this area became a magnet to the wealthy, and several of the finest homes from that era are open to the public. They include Dumbarton Oaks and Marjorie Merriweather Post's elegant Hillwood Estate and gardens, both of which have extensive art collections and elaborate gardens.

Preceding page: The White House South Portico is the world's most famous front porch

Right: Primates hanging about at the National Zoological Park

At Your Leisure

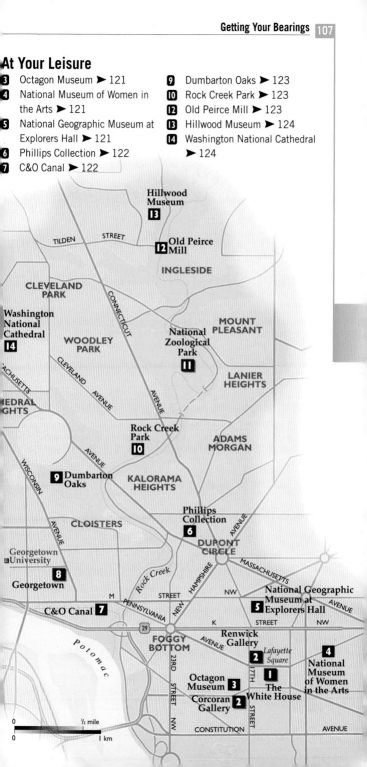

Drop by the world's most famous address and then take in great art, lively Georgetown and a visit with two playful pandas

The White House and the North in Two Days

Day One

Morning

If you have approval for a ❶ **White House** tour, meet at the appointed time at the Southeast Entrance. If not, take a lap around the White House, pausing at the South Portico and North Portico. Explore Lafayette Square, then walk east to ❷ **Renwick Gallery** (► 115) and spend the morning admiring the art.

Lunch

Try the Café des Artistes in the atrium of the Corcoran Gallery of Art (► 115).

Afternoon

Walk a block south on 17th Street to the ❸ **Corcoran Gallery of Art** (► 115). You could easily spend hours here, but today you're on a schedule. The highlights include 17th- to 19th-century Dutch art and 19th-century French

Impressionists on the first floor and 19th-century American art on the second floor. Then drive, cab or ride the Metro to Dupont Circle and the **6** **Phillips Collection** (below left, Renoir's *Luncheon of the Boating Party*, ➤ 122).

Day Two

Morning

There is no Metro station to **8** **Georgetown** (➤ 116–117), so you have to take a cab. Have it drop you off at Washington Harbor, where you can stroll around enjoying the fountains and take a short amble along the riverfront boardwalk. Then walk up Thomas Jefferson Street, where you can admire (and perhaps explore) the historic **7** **C&O Canal** (above, ➤ 122–123), before heading uphill to the shops and excitement of M Street and Wisconsin Avenue.

Lunch

There are plenty of restaurants to choose from here. One recommendation is to try the smoked ribs or chicken at Old Glory, 3139 M Street N.W.

Afternoon

Drive, take a cab or ride the Metro north to the **11** **National Zoological Park** (which everyone just calls the zoo, ➤ 119–120). Highlights here include the pandas (left, Tian Tian and Mei Xiang), Amazonia and the Great Ape House. There's lots of walking required, so plan some time out on a park bench, or at the Mane Restaurant at the east end of the zoo.

❶

The White House

More than America's most famous residence, the White House is recognized by many millions of people, rich or poor, living in every corner of the globe. Used as a visual backdrop for everything from CNN news to Hollywood movies and *Doonesbury* comic strips, the White House has become a universal symbol of America and the U.S. presidency.

Few people understand the complex roles that this single building has to play. In addition to being the personal residence of the president and his family, it contains the presidential offices and plays host to a dazzling array of state dinners, parties and political functions. It is also a national museum and one of Washington's most popular tourist attractions.

Many people are surprised by its small size. **Pierre L'Enfant**'s original plan for the city included a President's Palace that was more than five times the size of the current White House. George Washington, who was no slouch when it came to enjoying the good life, supported L'Enfant's plan. Thomas Jefferson and others, however, felt that the American people would not stand for a palace. They decided to hold a contest to attract a variety of less pretentious designs. (Jefferson wanted a modest mansion set in the beauty of nature.

Some White House Firsts

- 1833: Running water (Andrew Jackson)
- 1848: Gas lights (James Polk)
- 1866: Telegraph (Andrew Johnson)
- 1877: Telephone (Rutherford B. Hayes)
- 1891: Electric lights (Benjamin Harrison)
- 1929: Electric washing machine (Herbert Hoover)
- 1933: Mechanical air-conditioner (Franklin Roosevelt)
- 1947: Television (Harry Truman)

He submitted a design under an assumed name, and was reportedly annoyed when he didn't win.) From only nine designs submitted, the winning plan came from a little-known Irish builder named James Hoban, who was strongly influenced by the architecture of Dublin's fine homes. Blending elegance with functional simplicity, his design has stood the test of time.

Although White House construction began during George Washington's time in office, the first president to live in it was **John Adams** – but his efficient wife Abigail thought little of the drafty, half-finished home they moved into in 1800. In 1814, with the house barely complete, the British army put it to the torch. The fire gutted much of the building, but the walls remained standing. Soon reconstruction began, and smoke damage was covered with white paint.

More damage came after the 1829 inauguration of **Andrew Jackson**, who invited his supporters back to the White House for a celebration. As liquor flowed, a near-riot ensued, with drunken revelers smashing dishes, windows and furniture. Jackson's staff spirited him away to a hotel, then placed large tubs of liquor-laden punch on the White House lawn and announced to the crowd that there were free drinks outside. As the revelers rushed out, the staff barred the doors and windows so they couldn't return.

Less damaging, but almost as rowdy, were the children of **Theodore Roosevelt**. They could often be found racing through the hallways, sliding down banisters and on more than one occasion riding a pony through the house. The boys were seldom disciplined, and in fact were subtly encouraged by their father, who took great joy in their pranks.

Teddy Roosevelt also was responsible for the first major renovation of the White House. Desperate for more space, in 1902 he had the East and West wings built as executive office space. William Howard Taft further improved the West Wing in 1909 by adding the **Oval Office**. But the largest renovation came in 1950. That year the building's structural problems became clear when Margaret Truman's piano began falling through the second floor. President Harry Truman and

Above: John Quincy Adams, the son of John Adams, the first resident of the White House, was the nation's sixth president

Left: The White House is both the president's home and office and is the top visitor attraction in Washington

Right: Harry Truman spent much of his residency in nearby Blair House while the White House underwent major renovations

his family were forced to relocate to nearby Blair House for three years while the White House was completely gutted and rebuilt with a new steel-frame construction inside the stone walls.

The White House Tour

The events of 9/11 brought heightened security and a change of procedure for touring the White House. Now, to take a tour you need to make arrangements at least 90 days in advance of your visit to receive approval (see box below). It is worth the effort, however.

The White House Library was originally a laundry room

The tours are self-guided and you begin in the long **East Wing Hallway** where you'll find changing displays on the White House. On the first floor, you can view three smaller rooms: the Library, the Vermeil Room and the China Room. The **Library** is furnished *c*1820, and is still used occasionally for presidential press interviews. The **Vermeil Room** is notable for its portraits of recent first ladies, particularly the soft, ethereal portrait of Jacqueline Kennedy.

On the second floor, you'll enter the large and impressive **East Room**. This room is used frequently to host large state dinners and both Abraham Lincoln and John F. Kennedy lay in state here after their assassinations. On the east wall hangs the famous "Lansdowne" portrait of George Washington by Gilbert Stuart, which was rescued by first lady Dolley Madison just a few hours before the British burned the White House to the ground in 1814.

Used for major state functions, the East Room was where President Theodore Roosevelt's children delighted in roller-skating

The next room is the **Green Room**, which Thomas Jefferson used as his private dining room. There are some exceptional paintings in this room as well, including an original Currier and Ives *Farmyard in Winter*, and a portrait of a bewigged Benjamin Franklin.

Next comes the **Blue Room**, one of two oval rooms in the original mansion. This room has been restored to look as it did when James Monroe had it decorated in 1815. Farther on is the **Red Room**, where Rutherford B. Hayes took the Oath of Office in 1877. The last major stop on the tour is the ornate and elegant **State Dining Room**, also used to host state receptions.

The Blue Room, where President Thomas Jefferson greeted the public after his wearing-in ceremony

How to Arrange White House Tours

The U.S. War on Terror has forced an end to walk-up tours. However, groups of 10 or more people may tour the White House from Tuesday to Saturday from 7:30am to 12:30pm if the tour has been pre-approved.

• U.S. Citizens: To arrange for tours you must contact your congressperson at least 90 days ahead of your planned visit. You will need to supply identification information (including birth date and place, and social security number) for all group members. If approved by the Secret Service you will be put on a confirmed reservation list and notified about 30 days prior to the visit. Even if approved, you should call the White House on the day of the visit to make sure it has not been cancelled.

• Do Bring: a government-issued photo ID for every group member over age 15.

• Do Not Bring: purses, handbags, bags, backpacks, food, drinks, tobacco, personal grooming devices, cameras or cellphones with cameras. No recording devices, no sharp or pointed objects, including pens, pencils, nail trimmers. There is no place to leave anything outside and if they reject an item you cannot enter until you are rid of it. Our advice is to carry only your ID and a wallet that fits a pocket.

• Foreign citizens: Contact your embassy in Washington prior to a planned visit. The procedure is as for U.S. citizens.

Thomas Jefferson used this as his office. The tour exits through the North Entrance, and outside via the North Portico.

TAKING A BREAK

After the tour, walk just one block east to the **Old Ebbitt Grill** (► 72) for grilled meats and vegetables; pasta, soups and salads at Ebbitt Express.

The elegant State Dining Room is used for more intimate White House gatherings

➕ 194 C4 ✉ 1600 Pennsylvania Avenue N.W. ☎ Tours: 202/456-7041 or 202/208-1631; www.whitehouse.gov 🕐 Tours Tue–Sat 7:30am–12:30pm White House Visitor Center (corner 15th and E streets N.W.) daily 7:30–4 💲 Free 🍴 Ebbitt Express: $ Ⓜ Federal Triangle

THE WHITE HOUSE: INSIDE INFO

Top tip Even if you don't have time to get approval for a tour inside the White House, it is well worthwhile to stroll around it. You can stand just outside the fence on both the north and south side, getting classic views of the North and South porticos. On the north side, take time to ramble around Lafayette Square with its green expanses and statues.

Hidden gem The White House Visitor Center has a wealth of displays on the history of the White House, and on the presidents who have lived there.

2

Corcoran and Renwick Galleries

The Corcoran Gallery of Art was founded in 1869 as both a college and a museum to house the art collection of William Wilson Corcoran. It moved to its present superb *beaux-arts* building in 1897, while its outgrown original home on Pennsylvania Avenue now houses the Renwick Gallery.

Corcoran Gallery of Art

The Corcoran blends masterful old canvases with sometimes radical modern art. Must-sees here include the **gallery of 17th-to 19th-century Dutch art** and the gilded **Salon Doré**, once part of the Hôtel de Clermont in Paris. **Clark Landing** has a unique blend of European and American art, including works by Renoir and Monet. The **19th-Century Gallery** has works by Mary Cassatt, John Singer Sargent and Winslow Homer.

Renwick Gallery of the Smithsonian American Art Museum

The Renwick (tel: 202/633-2850, Pennsylvania Avenue at 17th Street N.W., open daily 10–5:30) displays selections from the National Museum of American Art as well as American crafts, modern jewelry and furniture. Its building is ornate, with portraits, velvet benches and marble cabinets.

The Last of the Buffalo, painted by Albert Bierstadt in 1889, was given to the Corcoran Gallery of Art by the artist's wife

TAKING A BREAK

The Corcoran's **Café des Artistes** serves lunches and light fare.

✚ 194 B4   ✉ 500 17th Street N.W.   ☎ 202/639-1700; www.corcoran.org
🕐 Wed–Mon 10–5, (also Thu 5–9). Guided tours Wed–Mon noon, Thu 7:30pm, Sat–Sun 2:30pm   💲 Inexpensive; under 12 free; free Mon and Thu after 5pm
🍴 Café des Artistes: $$ Ⓜ Farragut North, Farragut West

Georgetown

Even before John and Jackie Kennedy livened up the cocktail scene by moving here back in the early 1960s, Georgetown had secured its reputation as the most politically connected enclave in the world's most political city. It was also young and hip. These days the hipness has largely relocated to the nearby neighborhoods of Dupont Circle and Adams-Morgan, but a list of Georgetown residents can still read like a who's who of American wealth and power. What you as a visitor really need to know about Georgetown, however, is that it is wonderfully historic, beautifully preserved, a fun place to shop and a great place to walk around.

Narrow, cobbled streets meander between elegant rows of historic (and unbelievably expensive) row houses. Clever shops on M Street and Wisconsin Avenue beckon passers-by, while the **C&O Canal** (► 122–123) offers a scenic walk that begins in the most historic part of town and enters a grassy park as it follows the Potomac. Georgetown was already a long-established riverfront community and seaport when the capital was moved here in 1800, and its handsome houses provided some of the earliest residences for the founding fathers. However, the late 19th and early 20th centuries saw the area deteriorate as a working-class neighborhood and eventually it became a slum. Its rebirth began after World War II, when Washington was growing rapidly, and the historic (and then inexpensive) row houses of Georgetown started to attract young professionals.

The dramatic architecture and fountains of Washington Harbor overlook the Potomac

Georgetown Highlights

Washington Harbor

Hardly historic, but delightful, this modern development is an attempt by Georgetowners to reclaim their waterfront. It consists of a broad plaza with gardenlike plantings and exceptionally beautiful fountains, surrounded by hotels, specialty shops and some of the area's better restaurants. This is a great

place for strolling or – if that feels like too much – just sitting on a park bench and watching the river traffic go by.

Thomas Jefferson Street

Between Washington Harbor and busy M Street lies the historic alley known as Thomas Jefferson Street. The architecturally interesting buildings here are some of the oldest in Georgetown.

The street crosses the picturesque **C&O Canal** (► 122–123). In the 1700s, the quaint row houses that line the canal were home to Georgetown's craftsmen and artisans.

Top: Historic row houses on M Street

Above: Washington Harbor and the Kennedy Center in the distance

M Street

This is the bustling and funky heart of Georgetown. Here, book-dealers, antique shops, boutiques, bakeries, cafés, and Thai and Vietnamese restaurants all vie for the attention of sidewalk strollers. One of the busiest spots is the **Shops at Georgetown Park** (► 130), an upscale, visually intriguing mall with a surprising number of one-of-a-kind shops. Next door is **Dean & DeLuca** (► 130), Washington's most elite grocers, where for a price you can buy anything from fresh morel mushrooms to rare vintage wines.

Famous Georgetown Residents

- Senator John F. Kennedy and his wife Jacqueline
- Robert Todd Lincoln, son of Abraham Lincoln
- Madeleine Albright, Clinton's Secretary of State
- Ben Bradlee, editor of *The Washington Post*
- David Brinkley, journalist and newscaster
- Herman Wouk, author of *Winds of War*

The Old Stone House

This simple stone dwelling at 3051 M Street claims to be the oldest house in Washington. It was built in 1765 by Christopher Layman, a Pennsylvania cabinetmaker. Today, the house looks as it did in the late 1700s, and is run by the National Park Service. (Ranger is on site Wed–Sun from noon–5pm; tel: 202/426-6851; www.nps.gov/olst).

Built in 1765, the Old Stone House is purported to be haunted by at least three ghosts

Northwest Georgetown

Northwest Georgetown, the retreat of some of the wealthiest and most powerful families in Washington, is a great place to walk, with broad, tree-lined streets leading past a variety of beautiful historic homes. Two homes are open to the public. **Dumbarton House** (not to be confused with Dumbarton Oaks, ► 123) is a stunning *c*1800 Federal period home (2715 Q Street N.W., tel: 202/337-2288, www.dumbartonhouse.org; open Tue–Sat 10:15–1:15). **Tudor Place** (1644 31st Street N.W., www.tudorplace.org; open Tue–Sun), built in 1816, is a grand neo-classic house; Martha Washington's granddaughter lived here.

TAKING A BREAK

There's a great variety of restaurants in Georgetown. Try **Miss Saigon** (► 102) at 3057 M Street, or drop into **Dean & DeLuca** (► 130) and create your own picnic lunch to eat beside the C&O Canal.

⊞ 196 C2 Ⓜ Foggy Bottom 🚌 32, 34, 35, 36, 38B, D2, D6, G2

⚵ GEORGETOWN: INSIDE INFO

Top tip Try a ride on a historic **mule-drawn canal boat**. The rides are operated by the National Park Service and leave three times a day. Tickets are available from the Visitors Information Office at 1057 Thomas Jefferson Street; tel: 202/653-5190; www.nps.gov/choh; open Apr–Oct Wed–Sun (admission moderate; under 3 free).

National Zoological Park

Covering 160 beautifully landscaped acres (65ha) originally designed by Frederick Law Olmsted, the creator of New York's Central Park, the National Zoo is one of the high points of any visit to Washington. In 2000, the zoo once again gained international headlines with the arrival of Mei Xiang and Tian Tian, two giant pandas – a gift from the People's Republic of China. Although the pandas are the zoo's top attraction, they are just one of many interesting things to see and do here.

Tigers and other endangered species are bred at Washington's National Zoological Park

Over the past 20 years, this unique facility has been transforming itself from a traditional city zoo into a diverse and exciting zoological park.

Some of the zoo's most interesting cutting-edge work is with the large apes. If you look overhead in the vicinity of **Great Ape House**, you'll see heavy steel cables that are an "orangutan highway," which allows the large red primates to move freely between buildings. One of the buildings they go to is the **Think Tank**, where you can watch them interact with scientists and work on learning language and computer skills.

Another example of the zoo's work has to do with one of the **smallest monkeys**. Walking along the trails, you may hear rustling in the leaves. No, it's not squirrels; it is the pretty little golden lion tamarin. They run free within the zoo as part of a program to reacquaint them with life in the wild, so that one day they may be released back into their native Brazilian habitat.

The zoo's popular attractions include **Amazonia**, an indoor enclosure that simulates an Amazon rain forest. On the first floor there's a large "jungle river" that contains several species of Amazonian fish, some up to 9 feet (2.7m) long. The upper level is a very realistic (and steamy) tropical jungle complete with dripping plants, howling monkeys, shrieking birds and a diversity of equatorial life.

Other favorite stops include the **Big Cat House**, the **Asia Trail**, the **seal and sea lion exhibits** and the **Reptile**

House, whose largest inhabitants, Komodo dragons, grow to 8 feet (2.5m) long and can weigh 200 pounds (91kg). The zoo also offers a regular schedule of naturalist talks, animal feedings and training sessions that take place throughout the day.

As part of the Smithsonian Institution, the quality of exhibits is very high and, best of all, admission is free (although you will have to pay for parking).

The site is on a steep hill, so comfortable shoes are highly recommended.

Above: Unusually for a zoo, the apes have the freedom to roam around on the "orangutan highway"

Left: A baby giraffe stays close to its mother

TAKING A BREAK

The **Mane Restaurant** is the best option, although it serves predictable food for crowds, and can be very busy at noon.

✚ 197 E5 ✉ 3001 Connecticut Avenue N.W., 2.25 miles (3.6km) northwest of the White House ☎ 202/633-4800; www.nationalzoo.si.edu ⏰ May 1–Sep 15 buildings daily 10–6, grounds daily 6am–8pm; Sep 16–Apr buildings 10–4:30, grounds 6–6 💵 Free Ⓜ Woodley Park, Zoo or Cleveland Park

---

NATIONAL ZOOLOGICAL PARK: INSIDE INFO

Top tip The best time to see the zoo is in the **early morning** when the animals are most active and there aren't yet crowds of people.

Hidden gem There is an excellent naturalist bookstore in the zoo's **Education Building** for those with a deeper interest in wildlife.

At Your Leisure

Octagon Museum

ctually a hexagon, this unusual
ansion was misnamed by its first
wner, Colonel John Tayloe. In 1814,
served as the temporary White
ouse after the British attacked the
ty. In 1990, the building underwent a
15.5 million restoration and reopened
s the Museum of Architecture. The
rchitectural history displays are
teresting, but really delightful are the
impses of the 19th-century lifestyles
f wealthy Americans.

➕ 194 B4 ✉ 1799 New York Avenue
N.W. ☎ 202/638-3221;
www.archfoundation.org/octagon
🕐 Call for tour information
💲 Inexpensive 🚇 Farragut West

National Museum of Women in the Arts

Vith 2,700 works by 800 artists,
his museum presents the finest and
host important collection of its
ind in the world. Paintings by
romen date back to the 16th cen-
ury, and there are also works of
ilver, ceramics, prints, photographs
nd decorative arts.

Portrait of a Noblewoman, painted by
Lavinia Fontana in 1580, can be seen in the
National Museum of Women in the Arts

One of the earliest paintings here is
the *Portrait of a Noblewoman* by
Renaissance artist Lavinia Fontana.
There are also works by Impressionist
painters such as Mary Cassatt and
Berthe Morisot, and 20th-century
artists such as Georgia O'Keeffe, Frida
Kahlo and Alma Thomas.

➕ 195 D4 ✉ 1250 New York
Avenue N.W. ☎ 202/783-5000;
www.nmwa.org 🕐 Mon–Sat 10–5, Sun
noon–5 💲 Inexpensive 🍴 Mezzanine
Café: $$ 🚇 Metro Center

5 National Geographic Museum at Explorers Hall

Founded in 1888, the National
Geographic Society has funded major
scientific expeditions to every corner
of the globe. The Explorers Hall
presents rotating exhibits that
highlight the National
Geographic's favorite themes
of science and discovery.
Exhibits are geared for both
young and old, and are updated
to match popular interests.
Many use the same stunning

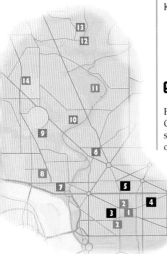

photography that made *National Geographic* magazine famous.

➕ 194 B5 ✉ 1145 17th Street at M Street N.W. ☎ 202/857-7588; www.nationalgeographic.com/museum 🕐 Mon–Sat 9–5, Sun 10–5 💲 Free 🚇 Farragut North

⑥ Phillips Collection

This charming retreat from the city was founded in 1921 by industrialist Duncan Phillips, who amassed over 2,000 works during his lifetime and donated his home as a gallery for the collection. It has since been expanded and renovated several times.

In the Gallery of European Masterworks, it seems at every turn your eyes settle on yet another masterpiece, such as Picasso's *The Blue Room* or Pierre Bonnard's *The Open Window*. Works by Cézanne, Matisse and Van Gogh can be found here, as well as Edgar Degas's famous *Dancers at the Barre*. But the most celebrated painting is Renoir's wall-size *Luncheon of the Boating Party*.

Another gallery contains works by artists that Phillips personally championed in the 1920s, including Milton Avery and Edward Hopper. A separate Paul Klee room contains several of the artist's most memorable works, including *The Arrival of the Jugglers*.

The Phillips Collection was America's first museum of modern art

Downstairs, the main house has even more art and an auditorium that hosts concerts every Sunday (Oct–May).

➕ 197 E3 ✉ 1600 21st Street N.W. ☎ 202/387-2151; www.phillipscollection.org 🕐 Tue–Sat 10–5 (also Thu 5–8:30), Sun 11–6 💲 Moderate; under 18 free 🍴 Café: $ 🚇 Dupont Circle

⑦ C&O Canal

George Washington was the first to dream of using the Potomac River as a highway to carry goods from the capital to the booming Ohio River Valley. But it wasn't until 1825, when the Chesapeake & Ohio Co. built a canal along the full length of the river, that Washington's dream became reality.

Today the whole length of the canal is a national historic park that begins in the heart of Georgetown and extends for around 155 miles (248km) to Cumberland in Maryland. There are two ways to experience the canal. The first is to walk along it, starting from Thomas Jefferson Street and continuing out of town to where the landscape presents pastoral views of the Potomac River. Or you can take one of the mule-drawn canal boat rides operated by the National Park Service.

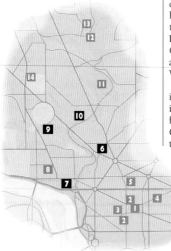

rom April through September, there
re three rides a day; they last about
) minutes and traverse at least one
istoric lock.

🗺 196 C1 ✉ C&O Canal Visitor Center:
1057 Thomas Jefferson Street N.W.
☎ Canal boat rides: 202/653-5190
🕐 Visitor Center: Wed–Sun 9–4:30,
Sat–Sun 10–4 💲 Free; Canal boat tour
moderate: under 3 free 🚌 M Street: 30,
32, 34, 35, 36

Dumbarton Oaks

uilt in 1800, this grand estate was
cquired in 1920 by diplomat Robert
Woods Bliss to house his growing
ollection of Byzantine and pre-
olumbian art. In 1940, he gave his
ouse and outstanding art collection
) Harvard University.

For years American, British,
hinese and Russian diplomats met
ere to establish the guidelines for the
uture United Nations. The mansion/
useum is undergoing renovation
nd is due to reopen in 2008. The
re-Columbian collection includes
tunning examples of Maya, Aztec
nd Inca sculptures, and gold and
de jewelry. Equally impressive is the
yzantine collection, with religious
rtifacts and decorative items. You can
njoy the estate's 10 acres (4ha) of
agnificent gardens, which include a
)se garden with more than 1,000
arieties of roses.

e rose garden at Dumbarton Oaks
rovides unforgettable aromas

🗺 196 C3 ✉ Museum: 1703 32nd
Street N.W. Garden: 3101 R Street N.W.
☎ 202/339-6400; www.doaks.org
🕐 Museum: closed until 2008. Garden:
Mar 15–Oct 31 Tue–Sun 2–6; Nov–Mar
14 2–5 💲 Garden inexpensive, Mar
15–Oct 31; free Nov–Mar 14 🚌 30, 32,
34, 36

⑩ Rock Creek Park

Rock Creek Park follows a wooded
gorge for over 10 miles (16km)
through the heart of D.C. Best known
for attractions like Old Peirce Mill
and the National Zoo, the park itself
is a lush green space with numerous
hiking and biking trails. There is a
visitor and nature center, and a planetarium that offers Wednesday and
weekend astronomy shows geared for
children as well as adults. Also within
the park are the ruins of Fort Stevens.

🗺 197 D4 ✉ Visitor Center: 5200
Glover Road N.W. ☎ 202/895-6070;
www.nps.gov/rocr 🕐 Daily dawn–dusk.
Visitor Center: Wed–Sun 9–5 💲 Free
🚌 Nebraska Avenue: D31, D33, D34,
W45, W46. 16th Street: S1, S2, S4
💲 Free

⑫ Old Peirce Mill

Built in 1827, Old Peirce Mill was one
of eight water-powered mills that
once operated along Rock Creek, and
it remained in operation until 1897.
This was one of the earliest mills to
use water power not just to grind
grain, but also to lift the grain to the
mill's upper floors, sift it and bag it.

The mill was restored to working order in 1936. Currently the machinery is undergoing a major renovation, but visitors can tour the mill grounds or join the ranger-led interpretive programs that are held twice daily.

➕ 192 B5 ✉ Beach Drive, just north of the Visitor Center ☎ 202/282-0927 🕐 Barn: Sat–Sun noon–4pm 💲 Free 🚇 Woodley Park, Zoo, Cleveland Park, Van Ness, UDC

🔟 Hillwood Museum and Gardens

Breakfast-cereal heiress Marjorie Merriweather Post bought the elegant Hillwood estate in 1955 as a show-place for her 18th- and 19th-century French and Russian art. The mansion underwent a multimillion-dollar restoration from 1997 to 2000. Reservations are required to visit (weeks in advance in summer). Guided tours are limited to 380 per day on a space available basis. The collection presents an outstanding array of French and Russian paintings, tapestries and decorative artworks, with more than 90 Fabergé pieces, including a Fabergé egg given by Czar Nicholas II to his wife. The 25 acres (10ha) include rose gardens, a Japanese garden and a greenhouse with over 2,000 varieties of orchids.

Statuary at the National Cathedral

➕ 192 B5 ✉ 4155 Linnean Avenue N.W. ☎ 202/686-5807; www.hillwoodmuseum.org 🕐 Gardens and museum: Tue–Sat 10–5. Guided tours: 10:30, 11:30, 12:30 and 1:30; closed Jan 💲 Tours moderate; under 6s not permitted on mansion tour 🍴 Café: $$ 🚇 Van Ness-UDC

🔟 Washington National Cathedral

Pierre L'Enfant's plan for the city called for a church at its highest point. But it wasn't until 1907 that Theodore Roosevelt laid the cathedral's cornerstone. The Gothic-style structure is more than 167 yards long (152.5m) and has twin spires of 301 feet (92m). The organ has 10,250 pipes, and there are over 200 stained glass windows, including one on space flight that contains a small piece of moon rock. Martin Luther King, Jr. gave his last sermon here five days before he was assassinated.

➕ 196 B5 ✉ Massachusetts and Wisconsin avenues N.W. ☎ 202/537-6200; www.cathedral.org/cathedral 🕐 Jun–Aug daily 8–8; Sep–May Sun 8–6:30, Mon–Fri 10–5:30, Sat 10–4:30. Guided tours: Mon–Sat 10–3:15, Sun 12:45–2:30 💲 Free: tours inexpensive 🚌 30, 32, 34, 36, N2, N4, N6

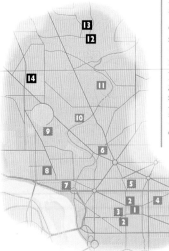

Where to...
Eat and Drink

Prices
Expect to pay per person for a meal, including drinks, tax and service
$ under $30 **$$** $30–$60 **$$$** over $60

RESTAURANTS

▼▼▼ Asia Nora $$$
Savor exceptional all-organic Asian cuisine at this serene restaurant decorated with Asian artifacts. Creative seasonal dishes capture flavors from across Asia with entrees such as sesame-crusted tuna with wasabi potato purée or sansho roasted duck breast with shiitake mushrooms. Save room for the jasmine and cardamom crème brulée.

➕ 194 A5 ⊠ 2213 M Street N.W.
☎ 202/797-4860 🕒 Mon–Thu
5:30–10, Fri–Sat 5:30–10:30

▼▼ Bistro Français $$
This casual bistro attracts a late-night celebratory crowd. Typical dishes include fresh fish, rotisserie chicken, venison and homemade pastries. Traditional French plates like *coq au vin* and *steak tartare* are served as well. A lower-priced three-course meal is offered between 5 and 7, and again after 10:30. The Sunday brunch with unlimited champagne is a local favorite.

➕ 196 C1 ⊠ 3124 M Street N.W.
☎ 202/338-3830;
www.bistrofrancaisdc.com 🕒 Daily
11am–3am (also Fri–Sat 3–4am)

▼▼ Café Asia $$
A variety of Asian cuisine is available in this trendy two-floor contemporary restaurant. The tasty entrees from across Asia are prepared with a contemporary twist. The Japanese sushi is popular, there are Vietnamese spring rolls, *pad thai* from Thailand, Chinese pork dumplings, spicy Indonesian fish filet, and noodle dishes, including Singapore noodles with shrimp and roast pork. There is also a selection of soups, salads and desserts, including combo banana and sticky rice.

➕ 194 B4 ⊠ 1720 I Street NW
☎ 202/659-2696; www.cafeasia.com
🕒 Sun–Thu 11:30am–11pm, Fri–Sat
noon–midnight

▼▼ Café Milano $$
Café Milano has long topped the capital's see-and-be-seen list. Respectable, if overpriced, Milano serves steak and seafood dishes along with thin-crust pizzas and homemade pastas. At night, the restaurant transforms into a cocktail bar, with men often dressed in Armani and women in Prada exchanging stories around the last table diners. Live music is sometimes offered weekend nights.

➕ 196 C2 ⊠ 3251 Prospect Street
N.W. ☎ 202/333-6183;
www.cafemilano.net 🕒 Sun–Wed
11:30–11, Thu–Sat 11:30am–midnight

▼▼▼ Cashion's Eat Place $$
Don't let the casual decor and moderately priced menu fool you. Cashion's serves some of the best food in D.C. and attracts a diverse, cultured crowd that returns again and again for Ann Cashion's inspired cooking. The dining room is simple and earthy, with hardwood floors, studio lighting, black and white art and a large semicircular bar that's the restaurant's centerpiece. Entrees, which change daily, are always fresh, organic and carefully prepared.

➕ 197 F4 ⊠ 1819 Columbia Road
N.W. ☎ 202/797-1819;
www.cashionseatplace.com
🕒 Tue–Sat 5:30–10 (also Wed–Sat
10–11pm), Sun 11:30–2:30, 5:30–10

Ching Ching Cha $

Just south of M Street this cozy Chinese teahouse has rosewood tables, sunlight streaming through the skylight and soft music. The menu is simple, with more than 60 varieties of tea, and small dishes to enjoy while you sit on soft cushions at the low floor tables while you sip tea. Menu items include steamed dumplings, curried beef in puff pastry and tofu in teriyaki sauce.

➕ 196 C1 ⊠ 1063 Wisconsin Avenue N.W. ☎ 202/333-8288 ⊗ Tue–Sat 11:30–9, Sun 11:30–7

Clyde's of Georgetown $

This is an old favorite around town, and more like an early 20th-century brasserie than a modern bar. Two dimly lit bars and a dining room with a fireplace lend an air of sophistication, despite nonstop sports on TVs. The menu is typical of an American grill, but includes some delectables such as Maine lobster and prime rib. The casually dressed clientele is typically Georgetown,

with a mix of high-society types, students and international visitors.

➕ 196 C1 ⊠ 3236 M Street N.W. (near Shops at Georgetown Park mall) ☎ 202/333-9180; www.clydes.com ⊗ Mon–Thu 11:30–10:30, Fri 11:30am–1am, Sat 10am–1am, Sun 9am–midnight

Felix Restaurant and Lounge $$

This chic New York-type restaurant has a large mural that includes landmark buildings from around the world. The modern American menu with Asian and European influences changes seasonally. Kosher-style entrees are served on Jewish holidays. You can listen to live music in the lounge most nights.

➕ 197 F4 ⊠ 2606 18th Street N.W. ☎ 202/483-3549; www.thefelix.com ⊗ Mon–Thu 5–10:30, Fri–Sat 5–11, Sun 5–10

Heritage India $

Traditional Indian cooking is presented in a sophisticated yet comfort-

able setting with distinctive portraits, rich colors, elegant fabrics and fine dinnerware. The menu offers enough variety to satisfy vegetarians and lovers of fiery hot lamb vindaloo, yet also provides specials such as strips of grouper in a distinctive sauce. The vegetable fritters are delicate and the breads are tandoor-baked. Consider the tapas-sized dishes if you want to taste more selections.

➕ 196 B4 ⊠ 2400 Wisconsin Avenue N.W. ☎ 202/333-3120 ⊗ Daily noon–2:30, 5:30–11:30

Kaz Sushi Bistro $

Enjoy the excellent sushi, but also consider the Japanese cuisine with a Western twist, which offers traditional favorites as well as unexpected flavor combinations. Try the tasting menu or daily specials, which might include miso-marinated sable fish, Asian-style short ribs, fried calamari with a cilantro (corinder) crust or flounder sashimi with plum sauce. The *bento* boxes provide tastes of a variety of dishes and are popular for

lunch. Premium sake, fine teas and tasty desserts complete a fine Japanese meal.

➕ 197 F1 ⊠ 1915 I Street N.W. ☎ 202/530-5500; www.kazsushibistro.com ⊗ Mon–Fri 11:30–2, 6–10, Sat 6–10

Lauriol Plaza $

This stylish two-story restaurant, with its towering windows and vaulted ceilings, offers the ambience of a modern café with considerable rooftop and patio dining. The Cuban owners present food from throughout Latin America, including *tacos*, *enchiladas* and *tamales*. Although the place is always crowded, service is warm and attentive. The bar is usually packed for happy hour.

➕ 197 F3 ⊠ 1835 18th Street N.W. ☎ 202/387-0035; www.lauriolplaza.com ⊗ Daily 11:30–11 (Fri–Sat to midnight)

Lebanese Taverna $$

There seems to be a permanent line here, filled with hungry fans of dishes such as hummus and falafel, kabobs with various meats, and entrees from the wood-burning oven. An open kitchen looks over the dining room, replete with Middle Eastern furnishings and palm trees stretching toward the domed ceiling. The patio is very popular, and it can get noisy at peak hours.

■ 197 D4 ✉ 2641 Connecticut Avenue near Calvert Street N.W. ☎ 202/265-8681; www.lebanesetaverna.com ⏰ Mon–Fri 11:30–2:30 and 5:30–10:30, Sat 11:30–3 and 5:30–11, Sun 5–10

Morton's of Chicago $$$

This national chain of top-quality steak restaurants attracts an elite dinner crowd. The formal wait staff present the marbling of the various cuts before you make your selection, with New York strip, filet mignon and 48-ounce (1.4kg) porterhouse being the signature dishes. You can expect the portions to be large and à la carte.

■ 196 C2 ✉ 3251 Prospect Street N.W. ☎ 202/342-6258; www.mortons.com ⏰ Mon–Sat 5:30–11, Sun 5–10

New Heights $$$

The contemporary second-floor dining room overlooking a tree-lined street certainly makes New Heights feel like one of the local neighborhood restaurants. Studio lighting and eye-catching artwork by local artists enhance the dining room, which attracts casual diners every night with a varied menu. The cuisine is innovative with an Indian influence. Your server will gladly take time to help you choose a wine.

■ 197 D4 ✉ 2317 Calvert Street N.W. ☎ 202/234-4110 ⏰ Mon–Thu 5:30–10, Fri–Sat 5:30–11, Sun 11–2:30, 5:30–10

Nora $$$

Hidden among the embassies and chic galleries of Dupont Circle, Nora is a charming boutique restaurant renowned for its organic cuisine and superior service. In an elegant brick house with wood-beamed ceilings, executive chef-owner Nora Pouillon has created a dining atmosphere that feels intimate and relaxing. The Mediterranean-influenced menu changes daily, but always includes a vegetarian dish as well as fish and meat entrees.

■ 197 E3 ✉ 2132 Florida Avenue at R Street N.W. ☎ 202/462-5143; www.noras.com ⏰ Mon–Thu 5:30–10, Fri–Sat 5:30–10:30

Obelisk $$$

Small and sociable, this relaxed restaurant offers excellent Italian cuisine. Each night the fixed-price five-course meal offers the creations of chef Peter Pastan to a full restaurant, so make reservations. Dinner might begin with an assortment of antipasti followed by a pasta course and then a main selection of mixed grill or sea bass in an herb sauce. Italian cheeses (optional course) and great desserts finish the meal. The wine list is excellent, and there is a full bar.

■ 197 E2 ✉ 2029 P Street N.W. ☎ 202/872-1180 ⏰ Tue–Sat seatings at 6, 6:30, 7, 8, 8:30 and 9; closed major hols

Occidental Restaurant $$

Right next to the National Theatre and the Willard InterContinental Washington, the Occidental has been treating officials, business executives and theatergoers since 1906. Oil portraits of recent presidents decorate the foyer, while autographed photos of past and present politicians, foreign dignitaries and TV personalities cover the walls. Rodney Scruggs's classic American menu focuses on fresh seafood and local, organic produce. The historic restaurant is just as busy at lunch and in the evening.

■ 194 C4 ✉ 1475 Pennsylvania Avenue at 15th Street N.W. ☎ 202/783-1475; www.occidentaldc.com ⏰ Mon–Thu 11:30–10, Fri 11:30–10:30, Sat 5–10:30

Palm $$$

The Palm is Washington's top power-lunch and fashion-din'

restaurant. Modeled after the original Palm in New York, "America's first steak house" continues to serve unparalleled steaks and succulent three- to eight-pound (1.5–3.5kg) lobsters. The curiously understated decor belies the executive clientele the Palm attracts, and the atmosphere is definitely celebratory. Hardwood floors, tiled ceilings and walls plastered all over with caricatures of past and present politicos create a loud but comfortable environment. Be sure that you reserve a table well ahead.

✚ 194 B5 ⊠ 1225 19th Street N.W (between M and N streets) ☎ 202/293-9091 ☺ Mon–Fri 11:45–10:30, Sat 5:30–10:30, Sun 5:30–9:30

▼▼ Pizzeria Paradiso $

This pizzeria is small and very popular and the wood-fired oven here produces excellent Neapolitan-style pizza with carefully prepared crusts. Try the Atomica pizza with salami and red pepper, or the Bottarga with lots of

garlic, egg and mullet roe. A good selection of salads, breads and desserts round out the menu.

✚ 197 E2 ⊠ 2029 P Street N.W. ☎ 202/223-1245, www.eatyourpizza.com ☺ Sun–Thu 11:30–11, Fri–Sat 11:30am–midnight

▼▼ Sea Catch $$

Live Maine lobsters waiting to be picked from their bubbling tanks greet you at the entrance to one of Washington's best seafood restaurants, in the impressive building that served as IBM's original headquarters at the turn of the 20th century. The outstanding cuisine is fresh, organic and hormone-free, including grilled seafood dishes like mahi mahi, monkfish, North Atlantic salmon, Chilean sea bass and black grouper. In summer, there's a romantic terrace along the C&O Canal.

✚ 196 C1 ⊠ 1054 31st Street near M Street N.W. ☎ 202/337-8855; www.seacatchrestaurant.com ☺ Mon–Sat noon–3, 5–10

▼▼ 1789 $$$

Considered among the most romantic restaurants in the city, 1789 enjoys an atmosphere of gentility that pervades its four dining rooms. The rooms of this Federal-style town house are clubby in feel, with English hunt prints, wood-beam ceilings and period furnishings. Spacious tables are adorned with fresh flowers. Haviland china service plates from Limoges, and brass pigeon lamps with handmade silk shades. The classically based American menu varies nightly, although the seafood and rack of lamb top the list. A jacket is required for the men.

✚ 196 B2 ⊠ 1226 36th Street N.W. ☎ 202/965-1789; www.1789restaurant.com ☺ Mon–Fri 6–10pm (also Fri 10–11pm), Sat– Sun 5:30–10 (also Sat 10–11pm)

▼▼ La Tomate $

La Tomate is the perfect choice for a casual Italian meal in Dupont Circle. While not every dish focuses

on tomatoes, the best do. Ruby-red tomatoes bring soups and salads to life, blanket fresh pastas and decorate plates of veal and other steaks. The restaurant is especially appealing in warm weather, when you can sit out on the garden terrace. Live piano music is offered Wednesday through Saturday evenings.

✚ 197 E3 ⊠ 1701 Connecticut Avenue at R Street N.W. ☎ 202/667-5505 ☺ Mon–Sat 11:30–10:30 (also Fri–Sat 10:30–11pm), Sun 11:30–10

▼▼ Vidalia $$

Named for the small town in Georgia famous for its delicious sweet onions, Vidalia combines country elegance with Southern U.S.A. comfort. The dining room is decorated with pale yellow walls and murals, hardwood floors, and maize linen tables with blonde-wood chairs and candle lamps. Chef and owner Jeff Buben's "provincial American" cuisine dazzles the senses with Southern favorites such as pan-roasted sweetbreads, shrimp and grits, and of course Vidalia's signature onion casseroles. Finish with a Georgia pecan pie or lemon cheese pie.

✚ 197 F2 ⊠ 1990 M Street N.W. ☎ 202/659-1990; www.vidaliadc.com ⊙ Mon–Fri 11:30–2:30, 5:30–10 (Fri 10–10:30pm), Sat 5:30–10:30, Sun 5:30–10

BARS

Washington's most popular bars are found in Georgetown, Dupont Circle, Adams-Morgan and along U Street. In Georgetown, bars and restaurants line M Street, but parking here is very difficult, so many people take a cab. You'll find that local university students pack these neighborhood bars.

Blue Room

This trendy nightclub in Adams-Morgan is one of the lively neighborhood's latest hits. It's more upscale than other local bars, with couches, candles and cocktails as well as dancing upstairs.

✚ 197 F4 ⊠ 2321 18th Street N.W. ☎ 202/332-0800 ⊙ Tue–Thu 7pm–2am, Fri–Sat 11:30am–3am), Sun 8pm–2am

Dragonfly

Just off Dupont Circle, this futuristic bar and sushi lounge attracts one of the best-dressed crowds in Washington. Sip a cocktail around the bar or grab a table for authentic sushi and sake (table reservations recommended).

✚ 197 F2 ⊠ 1215 Connecticut Avenue at Dupont Circle N.W. ☎ 202/331-1775 ⊙ Mon–Fri 5:30–1am (also Fri 1–2am), Sat–Sun 6pm–1am (also Sat 1–2am)

Habana Village

The city's best Latin bar has three floors, one offering Cuban food, another relaxing couches and music, and the third a crowded dance floor pulsating with salsa and merengue aficionados. Dance classes, ranging from salsa to merengue, cha cha cha, and tango, are offered Wednesday to Saturday at 7:30pm.

✚ 197 F4 ⊠ 1834 Columbia Road N.W. ☎ 202/462-6310 ⊙ Wed–Sat 6:30pm–2am

Martin's Tavern

Drop by for a drink and a chat with Billy Martin, the fourth-generation owner who's often behind the bar, or one of his equally sociable staff. The quaint, warmly lit bar is a cozy respite in this high-powered city.

✚ 196 C2 ⊠ 1264 Wisconsin Avenue N.W. ☎ 202/333-7370 ⊙ Mon–Fri 10am–1:30am (also Fri 1:30–2:30am), Sun–Sun 8am–1:30am (also Sat 1:30–2:30am)

Mr. Smith's

Known as "the friendliest saloon in town," this is a live piano bar where crowds come to sing around the piano. Live bands play upstairs at night on the weekends, and there's a good café-restaurant in back.

✚ 196 C2 ⊠ 3104 M Street N.W. ☎ 202/333-3104 ⊙ Mon–Sat 11:30am–1:30am (also Fri–Sat 1:30–2:30am), Sun 11am–2am

Nathans

This 30-year-old bar with the look of an old boys' club stands on the busiest corner of Georgetown. Smoke a cigar and watch the game at the bar, or dance the night away in the equestrian-themed dining room, where the tables are cleared out for an after-dinner disco on weekends.

✚ 196 C2 ⊠ Wisconsin and M streets N.W. ☎ 202/338-2000 ⊙ Mon–Fri noon–11, Sat–Sun 10am–11pm

Third Edition

Larger than most Georgetown bars, Third Edition attracts the under-35 crowd. The bar itself is classic Georgetown dark wood and leather, but upstairs are several dance floors and an outdoor tiki bar. A DJ plays Top 40 and dance music Wednesdays through Saturdays.

Dean & DeLuca

The produce is so good here that it's worth a special trip, both to the café and the gourmet food store. Along with sandwiches, boxed lunches, coffees and teas, the café offers miniature French pastries, brownies, tea cookies and a host of other delights.

✦

🔢 196 B1 🖂 3276 M Street N.W.
☎ 202/342-2500 ⏰ Mon–Sat 8–8

Jolt N Bolt

Dupont Circle residents flock here for caffeine boosts as well as muffins, bagels, cakes, scones, sandwiches and smoothies.

🔢 197 F3 🖂 1918 18th Street N.W.
☎ 202/232-0077 ⏰ Mon–Fri
7:30am–11pm, Sat–Sun 8am–midnight

🔢 196 C2 🖂 1218 Wisconsin
Avenue N.W. ☎ 202/333-3700
⏰ Mon–Fri 5pm–2am (also Fri
2–3am), Sat–Sun 11:30am–2am (also
Sat 2–3am)

CAFES

Kramerbooks & Afterwards Café

The café in this famous bookstore gives Washington's intellectual elite another reason to linger. The American menu also has cocktails and a variety of drinks based on coffee. Weekend nights usually bring live music.

🔢 197 E3 🖂 1517/21 Connecticut
Avenue N.W. ☎ 202/387-1400
⏰ Fri–Sat 24 hours, Sun–Thu
7:30am–1am

Tryst

A fashionable café, Tryst caters to young professionals who come here to lounge in the oversized couches and chairs. Soups, sandwiches and salads are served along with espresso drinks, teas and cocktails. Not somewhere for peace and quiet as the crowds keep the noise level high.

🔢 197 F4 🖂 2459 18th Street at
Columbia N.W. ☎ 202/232-5500
⏰ Mon–Thu 6:30am–2am, Fri–Sat
6:30am–3am, Sun 7am–2am

Where to... Shop

GEORGETOWN

Georgetown is Washington's best shopping neighborhood. From the **Shops at Georgetown Park** mall (3222 M Street N.W.), with its designer clothing stores and accessory boutiques, to the fashionable shops lining M Street, you could easily spend a day browsing the area. Here you will find antique shops and art galleries, clothing stores and crafts boutiques, restaurants, cafés and ice-cream parlors all set amid some of the most beautiful Colonial town houses in the city.

Clothes and Shoes

For a good selection of fine clothing and shoes, a number of designer Italian and American stores border M Street and Wisconsin Avenue and are also found in the Shops at Georgetown Park mall.

Betsey Johnson (1319 Wisconsin Avenue N.W.), frequented largely by younger women, offers colorful dresses, skirts and tops.

An offbeat, almost punky alternative for both men's and women's apparel is **Commander Salamander** (1420 Wisconsin Avenue N.W.).

For shoes, **Prince and Princess** (1400 Wisconsin Avenue N.W.) is popular with men and women.

Antiques and Gifts

Susquehanna (3216 O Street N.W.) is one of the city's biggest and finest antique shops.

Gore Dean Antiques (3338 M Street) sell antique and new furniture and housewares in a 1940s-style department store.

Eight modern and international art galleries, the "**Canal Street Galleries**," are located next to the Sea Catch Restaurant (▶ 128) at 31st and M Street N.W.

Books

The three-story mega-bookstore **Barnes & Noble** (3040 M Street N.W.) sells nearly every book in print and has its own café. **Travel Books & Language Center Inc.** (4437 Wisconsin Avenue N.W.) offers guidebooks, travel narratives, language aids, foreign-language literature and travel accessories.

Food

Dean & DeLuca (3276 M Street N.W.), next to the Shops at Georgetown Park mall, is the city's finest gourmet market, with outstanding produce, excellent meats, specialty cheeses and an extensive selection of wines and champagnes.

DUPONT CIRCLE

After Georgetown, Dupont Circle is the city's best shopping neighborhood, known for its specialty shops, art galleries (found on R Street), music and bookstores, and cafés. There are a number of upscale stores are along Connecticut Avenue south of Dupont Circle, while the more offbeat stores lie north of the circle.

Gifts

Claude Taylor Photography (1627 Connecticut Avenue N.W.) sells travel photographs and posters, especially of France and Italy, and Tintin merchandise. At **Home Rule** (1807 14th Street N.W.) you'll find a selection of unique housewares for kitchen, bath and office. **The Proper Topper** (1350 Connecticut Avenue N.W.) has a quirky selection of whimsical hats as well as jewelry, clothing, handbags, martini glasses and silver chopsticks. **Burdick Gallery of Inuit Art** (2114 R Street N.W.) offers Canadian Inuit sculpture and prints of Arctic wildlife, family life and shamanistic traditions in all price ranges.

Books

No place gets more attention than **Kramerbooks** (1517–21 Connecticut Avenue N.W.), the intellectual haunt of Dupont Circle, open 24 hours on weekends.

Food

When hunger strikes, visit **Pizzeria Paradiso** (2029 P Street N.W.) for pizzas, salads and panini sandwiches with fresh ingredients.

With a real hearthstone oven imported all the way from France, **Marvelous Market** (1511 Connecticut Avenue N.W.) serves the best baked goods in town.

Clothing

Burberry (1155 Connecticut Avenue N.W.) is near by to **Brooks Brothers** (1201 Connecticut Avenue N.W.) both sell fine suits and other men's apparel. For women, **Betsy Fisher** (1224 Connecticut Avenue N.W.) offers a fashionable line of clothing.

Children

Kid's Closet (1226 Connecticut Avenue N.W.) sells children's clothes and toys.

ADAMS-MORGAN

Adams-Morgan has a variety of eclectic shops near the corner of 18th Street and Columbia Road, with most selling African and Latin American arts and crafts. The diverse neighborhood is an ideal shopping area for those seeking inexpensive and offbeat items.

The most interesting antique shop is **Chenonceau Antiques** (2314 18th Street N.W.), open weekends only. **Kobos** (2444 18th Street N.W.) has African clothing and accessories, and **Shake Your Booty** (2439 18th Street N.W.) trendy shoes. On Saturday mornings, there is a small **outdoor market** here where vendors sell Latin American crafts and some produce. Try **Daisy's** (1814 Adams Mill Road N.W.) for unique, funky fashions from New York – and, on the last Friday of the month, free champagne and chocolate. Next door, **Miss Pixie's** (2473 18th Street) has an amusing selection of high-quality retro furniture and art.

Where to...
Be Entertained

John F. Kennedy Center for the Performing Arts

D.C.'s premier performing arts center offers a range of world-class cultural experiences, including **musicals** and **children's theater.**

The season for the **National Symphony Orchestra** (tel: 202/416-8100) is September through June (in summer the NSO performs at **Wolf Trap Farm Park** in Virginia, ▶ 29). Free concerts are held daily at 6pm at the **Millennium Stage** in the Kennedy Center's Grand Foyer (2700 F Street N.W., tel: 202/416-8340).

The **Choral Arts Society of Washington** (tel: 202/244-3669) presents everything from Renaissance chamber music to Stravinsky's Mass.

Washington National Opera (tel: 202/295-2400), now directed by Placido Domingo, performs all year. Most seats are reserved, but check for late cancellations.

The **Washington Ballet** (tel: 202/467-4600) performs all year in the Eisenhower Theater.

THEATER

National Theatre
Here are D.C.'s biggest productions, including touring Broadway shows.
🚼 194 C4 ☒ 1321 Pennsylvania Avenue N.W. ☎ 202/628-6161

Woolly Mammoth Theatre
D.C.'s most respected alternative theater presents offbeat and occasionally controversial productions.
🚼 195 E4 ☒ 641 D Street N.W. ☎ 202/393-3939

Studio Theater
Studio's two innovative theaters are known for artistic excellence and award-winning acting.
🚼 194 off C5 ☒ 1501 14th Street N.W. ☎ 202/332-3300

MUSIC

Blues Alley
The city's best R&B and jazz club draws its inspiration from Duke Ellington. Steve Tyrell, Maynard Ferguson, Najee and the Count Basie Orchestra perform here.
🚼 196 C1 ☒ 1073 Wisconsin Avenue N.W. ☎ 202/337-4141

DC9
Mix of local and national acts, with live music and DJ shows, on the second floor. Ground floor for cocktails and jukebox music.
🚼 197 off F3 ☒ 1940 9th Street N.W. ☎ 202/483-5000

9:30 Club
This cool club gets big-name American and international pop artists.
🚼 195 off E5 ☒ 815 V Street N.W. ☎ 202/393-0930

DANCE

Joy of Motion
Various troupes perform styles from modern to flamenco, jazz and tap.
🚼 196 off A5 ☒ 5207 Wisconsin Avenue N.W. ☎ 202/362-3042

COMEDY

D.C. Improv
The Improv hosts nationally recognized comedians, many seen on TV.
🚼 197 F2 ☒ 1140 Connecticut Avenue N.W. ☎ 202/296-7008

MOVIES

Uptown Theater
This art deco theater has one screen.
🚼 197 off D5 ☒ 3426 Connecticut Avenue N.W. ☎ 202/966-8805

The Capitol
and Eastern D.C.

Getting Your Bearings

Eastern Washington is a study in contrasts. Capitol Hill is home to Congress, the Supreme Court and the homes of many of Washington's elite. Known locally as "The Hill," the area has a rich architectural mix of Federal, Renaissance and Classical-style government buildings, beyond which lie quiet, tree-shaded streets lined with historic Georgian town houses.

To the north lies Union Station, the vibrantly renovated train station that is now a bustling shopping center. To the south is Eastern Market, the largest of Washington's original open-air markets. Just a few blocks east are some of Washington's scruffiest and most crime-plagued neighborhoods. However, a number of the area's most beautiful and interesting attractions lie within or just beyond these neighborhoods. In Anacostia there is Cedar Hill, the home of abolitionist leader Frederick Douglass, and the Smithsonian's Anacostia Museum, which highlights African-American culture and history. To the north are Anacostia Park, Kenilworth Aquatic Gardens and the National Arboretum. For safety reasons, do not travel on foot, but take a cab when visiting these interesting and beautiful sites.

Preceding page: The Capitol is both a building and a work of art

Left: Cedar Hill was the elegant home of statesman Frederick Douglass

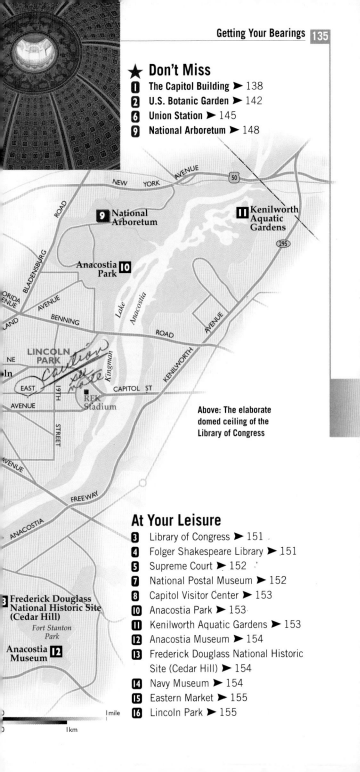

★ **Don't Miss**

9 National Arboretum

11 Kenilworth Aquatic Gardens

Anacostia Park **10**

BLADENSBURG

NEW YORK AVENUE

50

295

ROAD

FLORIDA AVENUE

AVENUE

BENNING

ROAD

Lake Anacostia

AVENUE

KENILWORTH

LINCOLN PARK

NE

LAND

AVENUE

In

Kingman

EAST

19TH

CAPITOL ST

AVENUE

STREET

RFK Stadium

FREEWAY

Above: The elaborate domed ceiling of the Library of Congress

ANACOSTIA

13 Frederick Douglass National Historic Site (Cedar Hill)

Fort Stanton Park

Anacostia Museum **12**

At Your Leisure

1mile

1km

Spend a day discovering the heart of American politics, then relax in some of Washington's finest open spaces.

The Capitol and Eastern D.C. in a Day

7:30am

Arrive early at the ticket kiosk for your timed tickets to tour the **1** **Capitol Building** (➤ 138–141). Tickets are distributed at 9am. If they can get you in right away, that's great. If your ticket is for mid-morning or afternoon, adjust the following schedule accordingly and/or spend a bit more time exploring the Botanic Garden or take a stroll around the lush Capitol grounds.

9:30am

Walk a short distance northwest to the **2** **U.S. Botanic Garden** (➤ 142–144). Spend about an hour here strolling through the conservatory and exploring the Bartholdi Gardens and the National Garden. While in the Bartholdi Gardens, pause for a while to appreciate the ornately crafted Bartholdi Fountain.

11:00am

Before you head down the hill to have lunch at **6** **Union Station** (➤ 145–147), you have time to explore one or more of the attractions near here. Choose from any of following: the **3** **Library of Congress** (above and left, ➤ 151), the **4** **Folger Shakespeare Library** (➤ 151–152) and the **5** **Supreme Court Building** (➤ 152).

Noon

The dining is fine at Union Station (above right). You'll find no shortage of restaurants here – at last count there were almost 50 to

choose from. You can slum it among the lower-level food court stalls to find such delectables as bourbon chicken, Japanese sushi or Chesapeake crab cakes. For more formal dining, there are several good cafés and restaurants on the upper levels. After lunch, plan to spend a bit of time exploring some of the 100 or more shops and marveling at the magnificently restored architecture of the building.

1:15pm

Take a cab to  **Frederick Douglass National Historic Site** (having made reservations for the tour earlier, ➤ 154). Drop in at the visitor center and watch the 17-minute video on Douglass' life. Take the 2pm tour of the house, and be sure to stop to enjoy the wonderful views from the front porch.

2:45pm

Take a cab to the **9 National Arboretum** (below, ➤ 148–150). Once there, take a tram tour if they're running, or pick up a guided map at the visitor center and head out on foot. Best bets include the Bonsai Museum, the native plant collections and, in springtime, the dazzling azalea collections. Spend a bit of time in the garden shop and enjoy the adjacent Friendship Garden.

5:00pm

The arboretum is closing, so let a cab return you to your hotel or to any of the fine dining establishments on Capitol Hill.

O

The Capitol Building

Rising in white-domed grandeur above the city skyline, the U.S. Capitol is one of Washington's most famous icons. It's no accident that the Capitol is visible from virtually every part of the city. When designer Pierre L'Enfant first laid down the city lines, he placed the Capitol building at its very center, with all roads radiating outward from it.

Although it took almost 100 years for the Capitol to become the building seen today, a century of labor has yielded one of the most beautiful and impressive buildings in the United States. But beyond the stunning architecture, there's a greater reason to visit the Capitol, for this is where the two branches of Congress – the **Senate** and the **House of Representatives** – meet to create and pass the bills that become the laws that govern the country. And here, anyone can step into the visitors' galleries above the Senate or House of Representatives chambers and watch the highest levels of American government at work.

The Capitol is both a working government building and a public museum. Walk up the broad marble stairs and step inside to marvel at room after room of fine marble columns, soaring arches, stone filigree, dazzling murals, vibrant floor mosaics, masterpiece paintings and elegant sculptures.

For a building of such grand design and intent, however, the Capitol had a less than promising start. To come up with a design, the founding fathers held a competition, receiving just 17 entries (none of which were appropriate). The competition was saved by a late entry from outside the country. **William Thornton**, a doctor from Tortola, was a friend of Benjamin Franklin's and a self-taught man who hadn't even thought of studying architecture until after he heard of the Capitol competition. He then studied day and night for months, and was astute enough to pay particular attention to architectural styles favored by George Washington and Thomas Jefferson.

The committee was delighted with Thornton's design, which had symmetrical wings extending from a tall, domed rotunda. With full Masonic ceremonies, George Washington laid the cornerstone for the Capitol on September 18, 1793. In 1814 the British gutted and burned the building, along with most of

Visiting the Capitol

Currently the Capitol offers docent-guided tours only from Monday to Saturday. You are recommended to arrive at the ticket kiosk by 7:30am (southeast corner of the Capitol). Tickets are distributed at 9am, one per person, so everyone going on the tour must be in line including children. The procedure will likely change when the Capitol Visitors Center (▶ 153) opens in 2007. Check the website (www.aoc.gov/cc/visit) for prohibited items, including large bags and sharp items.

The Capitol's dramatic dome makes it one of the world's most recognized buildings

Washington, and for the next four years Congress was forced to meet in a hastily built brick structure near by while the Capitol was rebuilt. By the 1850s, new, larger chambers were added onto the North and South wings. The dome you see today, in fact the building's third, was completed in 1866.

The Rotunda

Loosely based on the Pantheon in Rome, the Rotunda is a dazzling space that blends the best of art and architecture, and is often used for ceremonial affairs of state. It has hosted several presidential inaugurations, and nine presidents have lain in state here. If you stand in the center of the room (which is also the geographic center of the city) and gaze upward, you can marvel at the **dramatic fresco** that covers the ceiling of the dome 180 feet (54m) overhead. Artist Constantino Brumidi completed this masterpiece in 1865, having spent more than a year painting it while lying on his back on scaffolding. Titled *The Apotheosis of Washington,* it features George Washington ascending to heaven, surrounded by 13 maidens representing the original colonies. Brumidi also painted the first third of the **frieze** that circles the Rotunda just below the dome, which depicts the country's history from the landing of Christopher Columbus to the birth of aviation.

Closer to earth, eight massive paintings (four of them by John Trumbull) portray **key moments** in American history, including the embarkation of the Pilgrims, the signing of the Declaration of Independence, and Charles Cornwallis's surrender to George Washington at Yorktown.

Three Museum Rooms and the Crypt

Three of the Capitol's most historic rooms have been renovated and are open to the public. The most impressive of these is the **Old Senate Chamber**. Here, elegant round skylights set in the high, domed ceiling cast shafts of light down on semicircular rows of polished wooden desks and the ornate raised dais of the vice president. In use from 1810 to 1859, this room

Top: Brumidi's *Apotheosis of Washington* **looks small from a distance, but actually covers over 4,400 square feet (396sq m) and has figures over 15 feet (4.6m) tall**

THE CAPITOL BUILDING: INSIDE INFO

Top tip Watching a live session of the House or Senate can be a once-in-a-life-time experience. To gain access to the House or Senate gallery requires a pass which you get from either your Representative (House) or Congressperson (Senate). You can call 202/224-3121 to contact the appropriate office. Non U.S. residents can take their passport to the House or Senate appointments desk on the first floor of the Capitol to receive their passes.

witnessed the "Golden Age of the Senate," when famous orators – including the triumvirate of James Calhoun, Henry Clay and Daniel Webster – gave brilliant, fiery speeches.

Meticulously restored in the 1970s, the room has been used for special sessions, such as the Senate subcommittee's debate on the impeachment of President Bill Clinton. Worth noting here is the **"porthole" portrait of George Washington** painted by Rembrandt Peale.

One floor below this room is the restored **Old Supreme Court Chamber**. This was the very first room completed in the Capitol, and it served as the original Senate meeting chamber until 1810.

Also worth a visit is the **Old House of Representatives Chamber**, a large semicircular room where the House met from 1810 to 1860. Today, it serves as the Statuary Hall. Tour guides will often demonstrate the "whisper effect" that made the room very unpopular with politicians. The acoustics are

The Capitol Rotunda is the starting point for guided tours

such that even the quietest conversation can be clearly overheard by someone on the other side of the room.

You should also visit the **Crypt**, the large round room that lies directly below the Rotunda. This room contains exhibits on the history of the Capitol Building, including a fascinating set of models based on the various plans that were submitted in the Capitol design contest of 1793.

TAKING A BREAK

Treat yourself at the moderately priced **Capital City Brewing Co.**(➤ 156) a bustling pub with tasty fare and a children's menu.

🚹 200 B3 ✉ 1st Street, between Constitution and Independence avenues, at the east end of the Mall ☎ 202/225-6827; www.aoc.gov/cc/visit ◷ Daily 9–4:30 💲 Free 🍴 La Brasserie: $$ Ⓜ Union Station, South Capitol

❷

U.S. Botanic Garden

When you're ready to escape the madding crowds at the Smithsonian, a lush green oasis is waiting to be discovered next to the Capitol. The U.S. Botanic Garden, the oldest such garden in North America, has as its central feature an elegant glass-and-stone conservatory housing tropical and subtropical plants from around the world. The adjacent Bartholdi Gardens were named for the sculptor who created the ornate fountain at its center.

The idea of a national botanic garden was proposed as early as 1790. But it wasn't until 1820 that Congress allotted the funds to begin the gardens under the auspices of the Columbia Institute for the Promotion of Arts and Science. Its charter was "to collect, cultivate, and grow various vegetable products of this and other countries for exhibition and display."

The first conservatory was built behind the Old Patent Office in 1844. Then, in 1933, a new conservatory was built beside the Capitol.

In 1997, a complete renovation of the Botanic Garden was begun. Some of the conservatory's plants were transplanted to Bartholdi Park (see opposite), though most were sent to suitable greenhouses. The four-year renovation included the complete rebuilding of the conservatory and the restructuring of all the plant exhibits, reflecting themes such as man's interdependence with nature.

Inside, the layout includes a **"Jurassic Garden"** of prehistoric plants, complete with dinosaur footprints. There are desert

The U.S. Botanic Garden was renovated in the late 1990s

Above: A green and tranquil escape from the hustle and bustle of the Mall

Right: Plants from all over the world are on display

Below: Even on busy weekends the gardens are often not crowded

plants, endangered species, an orchid display and a tropical rain forest.

A 3-acre (1.2ha) **National Garden** begun in 2001 adjacent to the conservatory features themed areas such as a water garden, a rose garden, a lawn terrace, a showcase garden of outstanding plants and a butterfly garden.

Be sure to enjoy the beauty of **Bartholdi Park**, where several demonstration garden areas represent practical landscapes for both urban and suburban homes.

At the center of the park stands the magnificent **Bartholdi Fountain**, which was created by Frédéric Auguste Bartholdi (who also created the Statue of Liberty) for the 1876

Centennial Exposition in Philadelphia. Bought by the U.S. government for $6,000 and erected in front of the Capitol, the 40-ton fountain was moved to its current location in 1877. Standing 30 feet (9m) high, it features nymphs and seashells. Bartholdi completed his theme of "Light and Water" by including a circle of gas lights. These were electrified in the early 20th century.

Bartholdi's fountain reflects the free-flowing natural style that gave birth to the art nouveau movement

TAKING A BREAK

If you'd like to rub elbows with the political elite, try the **Hawk 'n' Dove** on Pennsylvania Avenue (► 158). Otherwise head for the multitude of restaurants at **Union Station** a few blocks away (► 145–147).

✚ 200 B3 ✉ 100 Maryland Avenue at Independence Avenue S.W. ☎ 202/225-8333; www.usbg.gov 🕐 Daily 10–5 🚇 Federal Center SW 🎟 Free

U.S. BOTANIC GARDEN: INSIDE INFO

Top tips The Botanic Garden is one of Washington's best-kept secrets, and in spite of its proximity to major attractions like the National Air and Space Museum, it is **seldom crowded**. Still, if you want the garden to yourself, try visiting when it first opens in the morning.

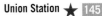

6
Union Station

This is no ordinary train station. In a way, Union Station is another historic monument, but one where you can sit down to a meal or spend hours shopping. If you enjoy shopping, Union Station will be a thrill. If you hate shopping, you can enjoy the wonderful restoration work on this monumental retail center and transportation facility, as well as view world-class exhibitions and international cultural events.

If you're hungry or thirsty, the choice of cafeterias, casual eateries and formal restaurants should more than satisfy your desires. With over 130 shops and restaurants, there really is a good chance you'll find something irresistible here.

And of course, if you want to catch a train, Amtrak and Virginia Railway Express are ready to serve you. Several major car-rental companies, including Budget and National, have branches here. And if you need a taxi, you've come to the right place.

For **women's fashions**, you'll find such shops as Ann Taylor, Chico's, Pendleton, Victoria's Secret and many more. For **men's fashions**, there's Knot Shop and Jos. A. Bank. If **accessories** are what you're looking for, there's Swatch, Bon Voyage, Claire's and several others.

There are shops selling books, music, toys, toiletries and lots more. Keep your eyes open and you might even see the president shopping around. In the **East Hall Gallery of Shops**

The main concourse of Union Station is a marvel of form and light

and Kiosks, there is the AMC 9 Theater, if you feel like resting your tired feet and watching a movie.

You can find American, Italian, Japanese, Chinese, Korean, Filipino, Mexican and Indian food in Union Station's restaurants.

B. Smith's restaurant (➤ 157) was originally built as the President's Suite, where not only presidents but kings and queens of other countries stayed, including King George VI, Queen Elizabeth II of England and King Hassan II of Morocco. In 1989, former President George Bush used it during an inaugural ball. But if you want to quickly satisfy your hunger or thirst with something less pricey, there are all the usual American favorites as well, from doughnuts and coffee to ribs and beer.

This magnificent structure, a fine example of *beaux-arts* architecture designed by Daniel Burnham, opened on October 27, 1907. But by 1981, when Congress enacted the Union Station Redevelopment Act, then-Transportation Secretary Elizabeth Dole had to develop a plan for its commercial development because it had fallen into such a terrible state. What you see today is the result of that three-year restoration project. Union Station is a bustling facility that serves more than 23.5 million passengers annually.

The scale of the building is awesome. The **Main Hall** is large enough to hold the Washington Monument laid on its side, while 100 feet (30m) above the concourse, the vast arched ceiling is a dazzling geometry of skylights and gilt.

Along the walls, marble columns support ornate archways, and inside and out there's a wealth of century-old sculptures and carvings that celebrate themes like technology, transportation and commerce.

Vital Statistics

- Style: based on Roman Baths of Diocletian
- Weight of Gold Leaf in Ceiling: 75 lbs (34kg)
- Cost: $125 million
- Cost of Renovation: $160 million
- Retail Space: 200,000 square feet (18,000sq m)

When it opened in 1907, Union Station was the largest train station in the world

TAKING A BREAK

For a quick cup of coffee, try **Café Renée** on the second floor.
Tasty light lunches – including a variety of soups and
sandwiches made with homemade bread – can be found at
the **Corner Bakery Café**. There are also several fine dining
establishments like the excellent **East Street Café**. On the
lower level, the **food court** presents a mind-boggling array of
fast foods such as burgers, Cajun chicken, sushi and dozens
of other choices.

🔲 200 C4 🖂 50 Massachusetts Avenue N.E., two blocks north of the Capitol
☎ 202/371-9441; www.unionstationdc.com 🕐 Parking and station open 24
hours. Shops: generally Mon–Sat 10–9, Sun noon–6 🎟 Free 🍴 Restaurants:
$$–$$$: hours vary 🚇 Union Station 🚌 80, 96, D4, D6, D8, X2, X8

The statuary in
Union Station
depicts classic
industrial-age
themes such as
"Commerce" and
"Transportation"

UNION STATION: INSIDE INFO

Top tip Union Station makes a great base for exploring Capitol Hill and the East
Mall. If you're driving, there is a large parking lot at the station and another nearby.
Within the station concourse there are 50 restaurants and more than 100 shops.

❾

National Arboretum

Virtually unvisited by Washingtonians and seldom discovered by tourists, there are days when you can feel as if you have the entire 446 acres (180ha) of the National Arboretum all to yourself. In fact, the only time it gets busy here is in April and May, when the gardens explode in a riot of color and a sunny weekend can see as many as 20,000 visitors. But even at busy times there are plenty of peaceful corners where you can claim your own small patch of verdant paradise. Time spent discovering its exquisite plantings and delightful gardens is well rewarded.

If you arrive by car, you can drive through the arboretum, stopping at the major garden areas to stroll and enjoy. Bicycles are also allowed, as is walking, but the area is almost too large for any but the most dedicated hikers to explore entirely on foot. On weekends from mid-April to mid-October, a fourth option is to take advantage of the 40-minute tram tour that will show you the highlights.

Several of the arboretum's attractions are within easy walking distance of the entrance, and among them are the following:

The arboretum offers year-round beauty, but it is particularly beautiful in spring

In the National Herb Garden you can see herbs that you've probably never even heard of

Visitor Center (Administration Building)

This elegant modern building appears to be floating on the surface of a still pond. It's a deliberate illusion created by the quiet water gardens surrounding the building. Inside are displays highlighting the arboretum's major attractions.

National Bonsai and Penjing Museum

Built around a core of 53 superb bonsai trees donated by the people of Japan, this collection has grown to fill four conservatories. The pagoda-like conservatories contain bonsai trees ranging in age from 15 to 350 years. Also on display are *suiseki* stones, revered in Japan for their ability to suggest natural scenes.

The **Penjing Collection** highlights the Chinese art of *penjing*, which blends miniature trees and stones in order to create diminutive landscapes.

National Herb Garden and Rose Garden

More than 800 varieties of herbs used in dyes, medicines, fragrances and spices grow in the National Herb Garden. Adjacent to the Herb Garden is the **Rose Garden**, which contains more than 100 varieties of heritage roses, and in early summer is the most fragrant corner of the arboretum.

National Capital Columns

Rising above a level plaza stands a Pantheon-like ruin of towering columns. The creation of landscape designer Russell Page, the columns came from the U.S. Capitol after a major renovation.

Arbor House

This attractive stone building houses a comprehensive museum shop, restrooms and vending machines.

The adjacent **Friendship Garden** is a formal area with an exceptional collection of perennials.

More Attractions

The following attractions lie farther away from the Visitor Center. You may want to drive or ride the tram to see them.

Azalea Collections and Morrison Azalea Garden

In spring, this is the most popular single attraction in the arboretum, when more than 12,000 azaleas and rhododendrons of every color and hue come into bloom. The azaleas blanket the wooded slopes of

Mount Hamilton, which rises 240 feet (73m) above the Anacostia River and provides unforgettable views of Washington.

Native Plant Collections

Top: It's easy to find a tranquil green oasis along the arboretum paths

This large planted area contains many varieties of native American shrubs as well as herbaceous plants. Highlights include the **Fern Valley Trail**, a 0.5 mile (1km) path lined with ferns and wildflowers; the **Grecian Love Temple**, which offers a romantic landscape of flowering crab apples and weeping beech trees; and more than 10 acres (4ha) of holly and magnolia.

Above: The Bonsai Collection is one of the best in the country

Asian Collections

This tranquil, narrow glen full of Asian trees and shrubs has a Chinese pagoda and overlooks the Anacostia River.

TAKING A BREAK

There are no dining facilities at the arboretum. Your best bet is to pack a **picnic lunch** and eat it in the picnic facilities in the arboretum's National Grove of State Trees.

🖪 193 E3 ✉ 3501 New York Avenue N.E., 2.2 miles (3.5km) east of the Capitol ☎ 202/245-2726; www.usna.usda.gov 🕐 Daily 8–5 🎟 Free; Tram tour inexpensive, under 4 free

NATIONAL ARBORETUM: INSIDE INFO

Top tips Even in spring, Monday and Tuesday mornings are **quiet times** here, with relatively few visitors.
• The area between the Capitol and the arboretum can be **dangerous**. It is recommended that you travel to and from the arboretum by cab or bus.

At Your Leisure

History, architecture and literature come together at the Library of Congress

3 Library of Congress ✓

Founded in 1800, the Library of Congress holds over 115 million items in 460 languages, making it the largest single library in the world. In addition to books, newspapers and periodicals, the library also contains artworks, photographs, maps and even a collection of Stradivarius violins. When the British burned the original library in 1814, Thomas Jefferson came to the rescue, selling his extensive book collection to "recommence" the library.

Although the library is now housed in three buildings, most visitors want to see the oldest and most beautiful of these, the Jefferson Building. Opened in 1897, the Jefferson Building is an architectural masterpiece of soaring spaces, mosaics, murals, sculptures and marble columns. The heart of this building is the magnificent Reading Room, where long tables rest among the stacks 125 feet (38m) below the great octagonal dome.

Some of the library's most interesting items are on display in the Great Hall and on the second floor, including one of only three perfect Gutenberg Bibles in existence, as well as treasures such as Walt Whitman's Civil War notebooks and Martin Luther King, Jr.'s original "I Have a Dream" speech.

✚ 200 C3 ✉ 10 First Street S.E.
☎ 202/707-8000; www.loc.gov
🕐 Tours: Mon–Sat 10:30, 11:30, 1:30, 2:30 (also Mon–Fri 3:30) 🎟 Free
🚇 Union Station, Capitol South

4 Folger Shakespeare Library

Founded in 1926, the Folger Library contains over 300,000 books, manuscripts, artworks, tapestries and prints, making it the largest single gathering of Shakespearean works in the world. The works date from the Renaissance to modern times and include the only surviving quarto of Shakespeare's *Titus Andronicus*, printed in 1594. Some

EQUAL JUSTICE UNDER · LAW

of the library's most interesting pieces are on display in the dark-paneled Great Hall. Guided tours are given on a regular basis, and include a walk through the Elizabethan garden next to the building. The library also has a traditional theater-in-the-round where Shakespeare's plays and Elizabethan music are performed regularly.

🔒 200 C3 ✉ 201 East Capitol Street S.E. ☎ 202/544-4600; www.folger.edu 🕐 Mon–Sat 10–4; closed national hols ♿ Free 🚇 Capitol South

5 Supreme Court

This elegant Corinthian building is home to America's highest court. Built in 1935,

The Supreme Court Building is one of the city's most ornate edifices

the building is a visual symphony of marble columns, painted ceilings, statuary, frescoes and sculpted friezes. Many visitors come for the architecture, but most come to witness the court in operation. Join the line and file through the Visitors Gallery for a three-minute look at the proceedings. The court is in session October through June (Mon–Fri, 10–noon, 1–3) and sits two weeks out of every month. The schedule is listed daily in *The Washington Post*.

🔒 200 C3 ✉ 1st Street and Maryland Avenue N.E. ☎ 202/479-3211; www.supremecourtus.gov 🕐 Mon–Fri 9–4:30 🚇 Capitol South, Union Station ♿ Free

7 National Postal Museum

One of the Smithsonian's newest museums, appropriately housed in Washington's historic Old Post Office the National Postal Museum traces the history of the U.S. Postal Service and highlights its importance to the nation's growth. Displays here include an exhibit on the Pony Express, a mail-carrying biplane, stagecoach and dog sled, as well as antique mail sorting equipment and an exhibit of fabulous and funny rural mailboxes. Another display exhibits interesting samples from the museum's vast collection of more than 16 million stamps.

➕ 200 B4 ✉ Massachusetts Avenue and N. Capitol Street N.W. ☎ 202/633-5555; www.si.edu/postal ⏰ Daily 10–5:30 🎟 Free 🚇 Union Station

🎱 Capitol Visitor Center

Scheduled for completion in late 2008, this mammoth underground facility will include an extensive educational center for visitors to the Capitol (and offer a great improvement over the endless wait in line to see the Capitol). The family-friendly visitor center will display famous historic documents, and present the history of the Capitol building. A virtual theater will let visitors watch the real-time proceedings of the House and Senate Chambers and interactive exhibits will focus on explaining the democratic process.

➕ 200 B3 ☎ 202/225-6827; www.aoc.gov/cvc ⏰ No opening information is available at the time of writing. Check the website or telephone

Safety

It is recommended to travel by cab to and from the Anacostia Museum, Anacostia Park, the Frederick Douglass National Historic Site and the Navy Museum because of those areas' higher-than-average crime rate.

🔟 Anacostia Park

On the banks of the Anacostia River and run by the National Park Service, 1,200-acre (486ha) Anacostia Park feels like a gigantic neighborhood park, with picnic facilities and trails. There is so much to do here, try out the golf course or the two marinas along the river.

➕ 193 E3 ✉ Recreation area entrance at the end of Nannie Helen Burroughs Avenue N.E. ☎ 202/472-3873; www.nps.gov/anac ⏰ Daily 9:30–5:30 🎟 Free 🚇 Anacostia (but best to travel here by cab)

⓫ Kenilworth Aquatic Gardens

Within Anacostia Park, this is the only national park facility in the country dedicated to the propagation and display of aquatic plants. Started in 1882 by amateur botanist W. B. Shaw, the site was purchased by the federal government in 1938. Today visitors can follow paths that meander throughout the 14-acre (5.5ha) facility past quiet ponds filled with lotus, water lilies and a host of other interesting plants. The gardens are bounded on three sides by Kenilworth Marshes, a 700-acre (283ha) wetland that includes a 1-mile (0.6km) walking trail from which deer, songbirds and waterfowl may be observed.

➕ 193 F3 ✉ Entrance on Anacostia Avenue, just west of I-295 ☎ 202/426-6905; www.nps.gov/keaq ⏰ Daily 7–4 🎟 Free 🚇 Anacostia (but best to travel here by cab)

A biplane permanently soars above a historic mail train car at the National Postal Museum

12 Anacostia Museum

This Smithsonian museum's full name is the Anacostia Museum and Center for African-American History and Culture. The permanent collection includes 7,000 items, and its traveling exhibits are first-rate. Examples have included The Real McCoy, African-American Invention and Innovation 1619–1930, and The Renaissance: Black Arts of the Twenties. Other exhibits highlight contemporary issues such as housing, education and health care.

🔲 193 E1 ⊠ 1901 Fort Place S.E.
☎ 202/633-1000;
www.si.edu/anacostia 🕐 Daily 10–5
🎫 Free 🚇 Anacostia (but best to travel here by cab)

13 Frederick Douglass National Historic Site (Cedar Hill)

High on a hill in Anacostia, Cedar Hill was the final home of famed anti-slavery abolitionist Frederick Douglass (1817–95), who moved here in 1877. Here you will learn the story of a man who lived a life of political struggle, intellectual passion and dedication to the improvement of the lives of African-Americans. Born a slave,

The rooms at Cedar Hill have been restored to look as they did when Douglass lived there

Douglass eventually escaped and with the help of friends bought his freedom, educated himself and went on to become a renowned leader of the abolitionist movement. His passionate writing and fiery skills as an orator won him many powerful and influential friendships, including that of Abraham Lincoln.

To see inside you must take a guided tour. Timed tickets are available from the visitor center, but advance reservations (call 877/444-6777) are recommended. The visitor center includes exhibits on Douglass, including an excellent 17-minute video that highlights his life and accomplishments. The house has been restored to look as it did when he lived there, and nearly all the artifacts are original. Among the items of interest are President Abraham Lincoln's walking cane, given to Douglass by Mary Lincoln, and a small writing desk that was a gift from suffragist and abolitionist Harriet Beecher Stowe.

🔲 193 D1 ⊠ 1411 West Street S.E.
☎ 202/426-5961; www.nps.gov/frdo
🕐 Apr 15–Oct 15 daily 9–5; Oct 16–Apr 14 9–4 🚇 Anacostia (but it is best to travel here by cab) 🎫 Tours inexpensive; under 6 free

14 Navy Museum

Tucked away 1.5 miles (2.5km) south of the Capitol is another of

Washington's best-kept secrets, the Navy Museum. This large and well-thought-out museum highlights the role of the United States Navy since the Revolutionary War. There are exhibits on polar explorations, submarines, space exploration and the opening of Japan to the West in the 1850s, as well as on each of the major conflicts involving the Navy. Items on display include a replica of the cannon deck from the USS *Constitution*, a bathysphere, a World War II fighter plane, and lots of big guns and cannons that you can touch. You also can tour the decommissioned destroyer USS *Barry*, docked on the riverfront. All visitors must call the museum 24 hours in advance for weekday visits and by noon on Friday for weekend visits (tel: 202/433-6879).

🚹 193 D2 ✉ Washington Navy Yard
☎ 202/433-4882;
www.history.navy.mil ⏰ Jun–Aug
Mon–Fri 9–5, Sat–Sun 10–5; Sep–May
Mon–Fri 9–4, Sat–Sun 10–5
🍴 Building 200: $ 🚇 Free
Ⓜ Eastern Market (but it is best to
travel here by cab)

⑤ Eastern Market

Built in 1873, this open-air market is one of the most entertaining places in the city to shop, particularly on Saturday, when the crowds can include senators and congressmen. Inside the large redbrick building, the aisles are crowded with traders selling flowers, poultry, fresh fruits and vegetables, gourmet coffee and more. There are additional stalls outside hawking everything from organic produce to antiques.

🚹 193 D2 ✉ 225
7th Street S.E.,
between C Street
and North Carolina
Avenue ⏰ Tue–Sat
7–6, Sun 9–4 🚇 Free
Ⓜ Eastern Market

⑥ Lincoln Park

Two powerful statues in this small urban park reflect important chapters in African-American history. *The*

Mary McLeod Bethune was a noted civil rights activist and teacher

Emancipation Monument, sculpted in 1876 by Thomas Ball and funded by freed slaves, depicts Lincoln reaching out to a freed slave who is rising from broken chains. Nearby is the sculpture of social activist and educator Mary McLeod Bethune (1875–1955).

🚹 193 D2 ✉ E. Capitol Street S.E.,
between 11th and 13th streets
⏰ Daily dawn–dusk 🚇 Free
Ⓜ Eastern Market

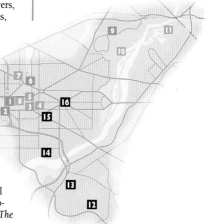

Where to...
Eat and Drink

Prices

Expect to pay per person for a meal, including drinks, tax and service

$ under $30   **$$** $30–$60   **$$$** over $60

RESTAURANTS

⯅⯅ America $

Dine at Union Station with seating in the bi-level dining room, train station lobby or along the outdoor sidewalk. A variety of American food is on offer, everything from full dinners to soups, salads and sandwiches.

➕ 200 C4 ✉ 50 Massachusetts Avenue N.E. ☎ 202/682-9555
🕐 Daily 11:30–11

⯅⯅⯅ Bistro Bis $$

Among Washington's many French-inspired restaurants is Jeff Buben's

Bistro Bis, on the first floor of the Hotel George near Union Station (▶ 40), an airy, open, Parisian-style brasserie. A huge zinc bar greets you and leads to the busy dining room a few steps below. The menu offers many recognizable French dishes such as *escargots* (snails) and duck confit, as well as more creative ones like pan-roasted sweetbreads with sautéed spinach, carrots, mushrooms and bacon in a mustard sauce.

➕ 200 B4 ✉ 15 E Street at 1st Street N.W. ☎ 202/661-2700;
www.bistrobis.com 🕐 Daily 7 – 10, 11:30–2:30, 5:30–10:30

⯅⯅ Café Berlin $

There's a lighter kind of German cuisine at Café Berlin. Peggy Reed and Irene Khashan, the restaurant's hospitable owners, are often seen chatting with their guests, many of whom are regulars. While you'll find *wiener schnitzel*, *sauerbraten* and *bratwurst* on the menu, there are also a number of low-fat main courses and vegetarian dishes. At lunch, the inexpensive soup-and-sandwich combination is a favorite of those in a hurry.

➕ 200 C4 ✉ 322 Massachusetts Avenue near 3rd Street N.E. ☎ 202/
543-7656; www.cafeberlindc.com
🕐 Mon–Sat 11:30–10 (also Fri–Sat 10–11pm), Sun 4–10

⯅⯅ Capital City Brewing Co. $

The menu at this bustling restaurant and brewpub includes traditional pub fare as well as regional cuisine. The food is far better here than is found at most brewpubs. The menu includes full meals, regional

favorites, daily specials, vegetarian entrees, sandwich plates and burgers, barbeque, fish and chips, salads and an exceptional chowder. The ales, lagers and pilsners are brewed on site, there is a children's menu and a good selection of desserts.

➕ 200 B4 ✉ 2 Massachusetts Avenue N.E. ☎ 202/842-2337
www.capcitybrew.com 🕐 Sun–Thu 11–11, Fri–Sat 11am–midnight

⯅⯅⯅ Charlie Palmer Steak $$$

Enjoy exceptional progressive American cuisine and fine American wines in a sophisticated setting overlooking Capitol Hill. The menu changes frequently and includes fresh fish, lobster, duck and chicken dishes in addition to fine steaks. Entrees might include grilled filet mignon with cabernet sauce or Chesapeake blue crab gratin. The all-American wine list is extensive, and includes wines from every state.

➕ 200 B3 ✉ 101 Constitution Avenue N.W. ☎ 202/547-8100,

a tandoori oven and served over buttery saffron rice, and skewered shrimp. Vegetarian entrees are also excellent. To accompany your meal, try *lassi*, a refreshing yogurt drink, or choose a wine from their impressive wine list.

➕ **200 C4** ✉ **301 Massachusetts Avenue N.E.** ☎ **202/546-5900**
🕐 **Sun–Fri 11:30–2:30, Sun–Thu 5–10, Fri–Sat 5–10:30**

BARS

Capital City Brewing Co.

Once upon a time this was a post office. Now it's a microbrewery with a restaurant and beer house serving the best brews in the city.

➕ **200 B4** ✉ **2 Massachusetts Avenue N.E.** ☎ **202/842-2337; www.capcitybrew.com** 🕐 **Daily 11–11 (also Fri–Sat 11–midnight)**

Dubliner

As might be expected, the Guinness is poured slowly and songs are crooned with fervor in

---

the Monocle's walls are covered with photos autographed by steak lovers like Bobby Kennedy and Richard Nixon.

www.charliepalmer.com 🕐 **Mon–Fri 11:30–2:30, 5:30–10, Sat 5–10:30, Sun 5–10**

Johnny's Half Shell $$

The seafood menu here is extensive, and includes not only fresh clams and oysters by the dozen, but regional favorites like Maryland crabcakes, Chesapeake bouillabaisse and fresh fish. Although seafood is the main focus, the menu includes beef and chicken entrees. The lunch sandwiches are large, with seafood, beef, hot dogs and burgers.

➕ **200 B4** ✉ **400 N. Capitol Street N.W.** ☎ **202/737-0400, www.johnnyshalfshell.net** 🕐 **Mon–Fri 11:30–2:30, 5–10, Sat 5–10**

The Monocle $

An institution since 1960, the Monocle welcomes both high-profile politicians and tourists. The menu is upscale yet simple: thick New York strip, fresh seafood and fresh salads. Operated by the Valanos family for over 40 years,

---

Two Quail $$

Enjoy romantic, fun-filled dining in a comfortable setting in classic Washington row houses. The service is excellent, with long-stemmed roses, privacy curtains and champagne on request for when you arrive. You can even arrange for an after-dinner carriage ride through town. The innovative American cuisine changes with the seasons, offering the finest in regional meat, fish and poultry. Selections might include two quail stuffed with pumpkin and appled dressing with Jack Daniels cider sauce, salmon in filo bathed in champagne sauce, or filet mignon stuffed with bacon and blue cheese. There is also a good wine list.

➕ **200 C4** ✉ **320 Massachusetts Avenue N. E.** ☎ **202/543-8030, www.twoquail.com** 🕐 **Mon–Fri 11:30–2:30, 5–10 (also Fri 10–11pm), Sat 5–11, Sun 11–3**

White Tiger Restaurant $

The White Tiger serves tasty Indian food like chicken baked in

---

B. Smith's $$

In the ornate President's Suite, built in 1910 in a gorgeous nook of Union Station, B. Smith's gives glamor to Southern cuisine. The popular restaurant has modern Southern dishes and an excellent liquor selection and offers live jazz on Sundays. Chefs Barbara Smith and James Oakley create gourmet versions of jambalaya, she-crab soup, Cajun paella and fried catfish.

➕ **200 C4** ✉ **50 Massachusetts Avenue (at Union Station) N.E.** ☎ **202/289-6188; www.bsmith.com** 🕐 **Mon–Fri 11:30–3, 5–9 (also Fri 9–10pm), Sat noon–3, 5–10, Sun 11:30–9**

this popular Irish pub that's part of the Phoenix Park Hotel (▶ 41).

✚ **200 B4** ⊠ **520 N. Capitol Street N.W.** ☎ **202/737-3773**
🕐 **Daily 11am–1:30am (also Fri–Sat 1:30–2:30am)**

Hawk 'n' Dove

Political types, lobbyists and lawyers frequent this bar near Capitol Hill, which has the feeling of an early 20th-century saloon. DJs spin their thing Thursday through Saturday at 9pm. The midnight breakfast can be appetizing after serious drinking.

✚ **200 C2** ⊠ **329 Pennsylvania Avenue S.E.** ☎ **202/543-3300**
🕐 **Daily 10am–2am (also Fri–Sat 2–3am)**

Mr. Henry's

Dark wood and stained glass adorn this Victorian-style pub which has been here for more than 30 years. Jazz quartets and cabaret acts perform on the stage.

✚ **200 off C2** ⊠ **601 Pennsylvania Avenue S.E.** ☎ **202/546-8412**
🕐 **Mon–Sat 11:15am–midnight, Sun 10am–midnight**

Scheisse Haus

German and domestic beers are featured here, and the decor enhances the Biergarten feel. There is a collection of European artwork, carvings and display cases filled with German *bier steins*. Seating is in booths, on couches or at solid wood tables with beer served in steins. Internet jukebox, billiards and TVs provide entertainment.

✚ **200 C2** ⊠ **319 Pennsylvania Avenue S.E.** ☎ **202/546-7782**,
www.pourhouse-dc.com 🕐 **Mon–Fri 5:30pm–1:30am, Sat–Sun 11am–1:30am**

Tortilla Coast

Popular with Capitol Hill interns, Tortilla Coast offers inexpensive Tex-Mex food and drinks. Happy hour is a festive, crowded affair.

✚ **200 C2** ⊠ **400 1st Street S.E.** ☎ **202/546-6768**;
www.tortillacoast.com 🕐 **Mon–Fri 11:30–10 (also Thu–Fri 10–11pm), Sat noon–10**

Union Pub

For tasty pub fare on the Hill, stop at Union Pub for burgers, wings, nachos, domestic beers and a relaxed atmosphere. Inexpensive happy-hour specials draw a lively (and sometimes large) crowd. Ten TVs monitor sports events. Why not sit outside on the patio and try the key lime pie?

✚ **200 C4** ⊠ **201 Massachusetts Avenue N.E.** ☎ **202/546-7200**;
www.unionpubdc.com 🕐 **Daily 11:30am–2am (also Fri–Sat 2–3am)**

CAFES

Banana Café and Piano Bar

Wacky and colorful, the Banana Café's interior decor is as fun as its food. Gaze at the Caribbean paintings for sale as you sip a *mojito*. The small neighborhood café offers good Mexican, Puerto Rican and Cuban fare such as tapas, plantain soup, salsa and seafood dishes. At night, locals dance as crooning artists play live music in the upstairs piano bar.

✚ **200 off C2** ⊠ **500 8th Street S.E.** ☎ **202/543-5906** 🕐 **Sun–Thu 11–10, Fri–Sat 11–11**

Le Bon Café

Grab an excellent espresso at this diminutive French café before heading across the street to join your guided tour of the Library of Congress.

✚ **200 C2** ⊠ **212 2nd Street S.E.** ☎ **202/547-7200** 🕐 **Mon–Fri 7:30–5, Sat–Sun 8:30–3:30**

Bread and Chocolate

This European-style café near Eastern Market offers hot main courses, specialty espresso drinks and pastries. Its wall-to-wall windows and location on a busy corner makes it an ideal place for people-watching.

✚ **200 off C2** ⊠ **666 Pennsylvania Avenue S.E.** ☎ **202/547-2875** 🕐 **Mon–Sat 7–7, Sun 8–6**

Where to...
Shop

Center Café $

If you're in Union Station, it's hard to miss the Center Café, a gorgeous two-level, circular restaurant smack in the middle of the main lobby. Though the acoustics are distracting in the busy marble hall, the bustle of travelers, commuters and shoppers is fun to watch. At inaugural balls, the Center Café becomes an island in a sea of bejeweled politicians; every day, it's a great oasis for a coffee break or bite to eat. The menu includes gourmet pizza, creative salads and desserts.

🚇 200 C4 ⊠ 50 Massachusetts Avenue N.E. ☎ 202/682-0143; www.arkrestaurants.com ⊙ Mon–Fri 8am–8:30pm, Sat–Sun 11:30–8:30

Cosi

Part of a national chain, this coffee-shop/restaurant – one of a dozen in the city – is designed to be a neighborhood gathering place for coffee, meals and snacks all day long. You can build your own sandwich or pizza and enjoy

espresso and lattes. This location, on a pleasant corner in Capitol Hill, has outdoor seating.

🚇 200 C2 ⊠ 301 Pennsylvania Avenue at 5th Street S.E. ☎ 202/546-3345; www.getcosi.com ⊙ Daily 7am–10pm

The Market Lunch

In Eastern Market, join the line for breakfast at The Market Lunch, which serves more than 1,000 breakfasts on weekends. Fast-talking, gregarious cooks shout out your order over a hot grill and expertly prepare omelets, blueberry pancakes, sausage-and-egg sandwiches – even crabcakes and the city's best North Carolina-style barbeque. A former *Washington Star* newspaper hangout, this place has been around for decades, and the food – along with the lively atmosphere – is well worth the wait.

🚇 193 D2 ⊠ 225 7th Street S.E. ☎ 202/547-8444; www.easternmarket.net ⊙ Tue–Sat 7:30–3, Sun 11–3:30

Murky Coffee

Students and government staff choose this espresso and coffee house that serves fresh ground drinks, great pastries and free WiFi. Sip a white chocolate mocha while you scan the Weekend section of *The Washington Post.*

🚇 200 off C2 ⊠ 660 Pennsylvania Avenue S.E (entrance on 7th Street) ☎ 202/546-5228; www.murkycoffee.com ⊙ Mon–Sat 7–9, Sun 8–8

Pete's Diner

Open at 5:15am, Pete's is an unpretentious Capitol Hill legend, serving traditional diner fare as well as tasty vegetarian specials and Chinese food. Early risers can catch the excellent breakfasts (which include Pete's own sweet potato pancakes), and researchers at the nearby Library of Congress often stop in for inexpensive lunches at the counter.

🚇 200 C3 ⊠ 212 2nd Street S.E. ☎ 202/544-7335 ⊙ Daily 5:15am–3pm

Union Station (▶ 145–147), on Massachusetts Avenue N.E. at North Capitol Street, is not only the city train station, but a grand marble building with two levels of shops and an excellent food court. Shops selling books, clothes, ties and toys are all found here. There are a couple of excellent restaurants and bars in Union Station as well.

EASTERN MARKET

Eastern Market (▶ 155), at 7th and C streets S.E., is a budget shopper's paradise, with a Saturday farmer's market and Saturday and Sunday flea markets where vendors sell everything you can imagine.

Where to...
Be Entertained

ARTS

Union Station

Changing art exhibitions in the West Hall of Union Station offer a respite for the travel-weary or shop-worn. There might be photographs of Barcelona, Rome or early 20th-century Washington, paintings, or something more unusual.

✚ 200 C4 ⊠ 50 Massachusetts Avenue N.E. ☎ 202/289-1908

MOVIES

AMC Union Station 9

This nine-screen movie theater is on the lower level of Union Station.

✚ 200 C4 ⊠ Massachusetts Avenue at N. Capitol Street N.E. ☎ 703/998-4262

THEATER AND MUSIC

Capitol Hill Arts Workshop

Local children and adults take acting, dancing and art classes here, but plays, movies (classics once a month on Fridays), and other performances are open to the public. Check the free *Hill Rag* newspaper, or visit the website, www.chaw.org.

✚ 200 off C2 ⊠ 545 7th Street S.E. ☎ 202/547-6839

Folger Shakespeare Theatre

Shakespeare's plays are performed October through May by various theatrical companies. The Folger Consort chamber music ensemble performs during the same season.

✚ 200 C3 ⊠ 201 E. Capitol Street S.E. ☎ 202/544-7077

---

olive-oil lotions. The two-floor store, open since 1978, even has a salon in case you need a facial.

ANTIQUES AND GIFTS

At **Antiques on the Hill** (701 N. Carolina Avenue S.E.), handcarved African statues are crammed next to grandfather clocks and antique jewelry. **Silk Road** (311 7th Street S.E.) sells vegetable dyed hand-woven Tibetan rugs, jewelry, prayer wheels and other Buddhist treasures. At **Art & Soul** (225 Pennsylvania Avenue S.E.), browse the eclectic, handmade line of clothing, jewelry and other crafts.

BOOKS

Capitol Hill Books (657 C Street S.E.) has an excellent and well-organized collection of used books. Inside Union Station, **B. Dalton Bookseller** caters to travelers and commuters with bestsellers, paperbacks and magazines.

Surrounding Eastern Market, which is easily accessible by Metro, are a number of bookstores, antique shops and clothing stores.

FOOD

Get your carrot juice fix at **Yes! Organic Market** (658 Pennsylvania Avenue S.E.), which also sells soy milk, organic fruit and vegetables, unique teas and healthy snack food. **Prego** (210 7th Street S.E.), an Italian deli and market, sells slabs of mortadella as well as European sweet treats like Ghirardelli chocolate and Nutella. Stock up on cold cuts and olives or order a salami sandwich to go and people-watch at Eastern Market.

CLOTHING

Ritzy yet friendly, **The Forecast** (218 7th Street S.E. across from Eastern Market) has a unique selection of women's clothing, jewelry, shoes, hosiery, soaps and

Excursions

In Old Town Alexandria you'll find narrow streets, alluring shops and restaurants, and tons of riverfront charm. Annapolis offers elegant Colonial homes and excellent waterfront eateries.

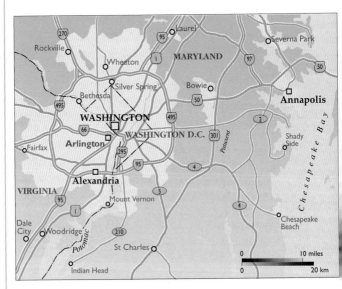

Old Town Alexandria

Long before Washington, D.C. even existed, Alexandria was a thriving trading port on the banks of the Potomac River. Since the 1970s, Alexandria's historic Old Town district has undergone an impressive restoration. Its attractive 18th-century stone town houses, narrow cobbled streets and lively waterfront marina make it a delight to explore on foot.

1–2

A good place to start, and to find a parking space on a crowded weekend, is at the **Lyceum**, a town museum on the corner of Prince and North Washington streets. The building itself is a fine example of Greek Revival architecture. Its early history is told in an interpretive display on the first floor.

From the Lyceum, walk east on Prince Street, turning north on Royal, then east on King Street and then south on Fairfax. A few steps down Fairfax Street stands the **Stabler-Leadbeater Apothecary Shop**. Founded in 1792, this traditional drugstore remained in

Preceding page: The Courthouse in historic Old Town Alexandria

peration until 1933, and counted George Washington and Robert E. Lee mong its patrons. Today it is open to he public as a small museum and gift hop that is worth a visit.

2–3

Continue south on Fairfax Street one block and turn east on Prince Street. On this block the **Athenaeum**, built as a bank in

lists the submarines on which it traveled). The factory is an art center with three floors of galleries and studios and works by over 200 artists. Go in and watch painters, potters, photographers, sculptors and jewelry-makers at work. They'll be happy to answer any questions. Also here is an archaeological museum that exhibits artifacts from several excavations in and around Alexandria.

4–5

Continue north along Union Street, turn west on Cameron Street, then south on Fairfax Street, and walk

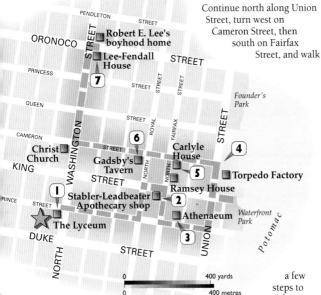

the 1850s, now serves as a gallery representing the work of the Northern Virginia Fine Arts Association.

3–4

Continue east along Prince Street, turning north on Union Street. At the corner of King and Union, an archway leads past some shops to the waterfront, where a boardwalk overlooks the marina and benches let you watch the river traffic. The boardwalk spans the front of the **Torpedo Factory**, which manufactured torpedoes in World War II (the green torpedo in the main hall was made here in 1945, and a log book tells its history and

a few steps to **Carlyle House**. This graceful mansion, built by John Carlyle in 1752, served as the headquarters for General Braddock during the French and Indian wars. A young George Washington served on Braddock's staff and was a regular visitor here. It was in this house that Braddock and five royal governors hatched the plan for the Stamp Act to finance his military campaigns, an action that helped trigger the American Revolution. Next door to Carlyle House is the **Ramsey House**. Built in 1724, this is the oldest house in Alexandria and currently is home to the Alexandria Convention and Visitors Association.

5–6

Head west again along Cameron Street. At the corner of Cameron and North Royal stands **Gadsby's Tavern** (134 North Royal Street), which was once a favorite haunt of George Washington. Learn about the architecture, history, arts, social customs, clothing and food of that period. The tavern and the City Hotel were operated by Gadsby from 1796 to 1808.

6–7

Continue west on Cameron Street for two blocks to **Christ Church**, which still reserves a pew for the Washington family. Turn north on Washington Street to Oronoco Street. Here, at 607 Oronoco, was the home of Revolutionary War hero Henry "Light Horse" Lee. It was here that his son, **Robert E. Lee**, spent his boyhood. The **Lee-Fendall House Museum** at 614 Oronoco, was once owned by Henry Lee's sister. It has been restored and is open to the public for guided tours.

TAKING A BREAK

Gadsby's Tavern (▶ above) is one of the few 18th-century taverns remaining in the United States. Downstairs, the tavern offers Colonial-style meals served by period-costumed staff; upstairs, guides take visitors on tours of the upper tavern rooms (which are purported to be haunted).

Alexandria was a busy port of trade on the Potomac long before the Revolutionary War

Athenaeum
✉ 201 Prince Street ☎ 703/548-0035
🕐 Mar–Oct Wed–Fri 11–3, Sat 1–3, Sun 1–4; closed Nov–Feb 🖐 Free

Carlyle House
✉ 121 N. Fairfax Street
☎ 703/549-2997; www.carlylehouse.org
🕐 Tue–Sat 10–4:30, Sun noon–4:30
🖐 Inexpensive

Gadsby's Tavern
✉ 134 N. Royal Street ☎ 703/838-4242
🕐 Apr–Oct Sun–Mon 1–5, Tue–Sat 10–5; Nov–Mar Wed–Sat 11–4, Sun 1–4
🖐 Inexpensive

Lee-Fendall House Museum
✉ 614 Oronoco Street ☎ 703/548-1789
🕐 Tue–Sat 10–4, Sun 1–4 (last tour at 3:45)
🖐 Inexpensive

Stabler-Leadbeater Apothecary Shop
✉ 105 S. Fairfax Street ☎ 703/838-3852
www.apothecarymuseum.org
🕐 Apr–Oct Tue–Sat 10–5, Sun–Mon 1–5; Nov–Mar Wed–Sat 11–4, Sun 1–4
🖐 Inexpensive

Torpedo Factory
✉ 105 N. Union Street ☎ 703/838-4565
🕐 Daily 10–5 🖐 Free

Annapolis

Annapolis, the capital of Maryland, was a thriving center of education, culture and commerce when much of America was still a vast wilderness. It served as the capital for a fledgling United States from 1783 to 1784. Many of its finest historic buildings have been lovingly restored, and the narrow streets are lined with colorful shops and galleries. Its marinas are chock-full of gleaming sailboats and powerboats, particularly along aptly named Ego Alley, where row upon row of multimillion-dollar yachts are docked.

1–2

On the highest point of land in Annapolis, the **State House** (State Circle, tel: 410/974-3400), with its golden dome, makes an excellent point of reference and a great place to start your tour. This is the oldest state capitol in continuous use in the United States. It was here that the Treaty of Paris, which ended the Revolutionary War, was ratified in 1784, and here also that General George Washington resigned his command in 1788. Free guided tours of the building are available daily at 11am and 3pm.

From the northeast corner of State Circle, walk northeast along Maryland Avenue. The elegant Georgian

Hammond-Harwood House, built in 1774 by William Buckland, has been carefully restored and exquisitely furnished. It is open as a museum that reflects the daily lifestyle of the well-to-do residents of Annapolis in the late 18th century, and is well worth a visit.

2–3

Walk back along Maryland Avenue and turn southeast on Prince George Street, following it to the **William Paca House and Gardens**. This large Georgian home was built for wealthy

The gracious dining room of Hammond-Harwood House

planter William Paca between 1763 and 1765. In 1901, the house was incorporated into (and the gardens were completely buried beneath) a 200-room hotel. Fortunately, the property was later purchased by the Historic Annapolis Foundation, and the house and gardens were carefully restored to their original grandeur. Today it is a museum with rooms full of period art, silver and special exhibits on life in the 18th century.

3–4

Continue along Prince George Street, turning west on East Street, and then southeast on Pinkney Street. The simple frame house known as

Annapolis has become the most popular yachting center on the Atlantic coast

The Barracks (43 Pinkney Street), originally a private home, was leased by the state to house Continental soldiers during the Revolutionary War. A few steps farther on is **Shiplap House** (18 Pinkney Street), which was built about 1715 and is one of the oldest houses still standing in Annapolis. It is named for the style of siding used in its construction, and was both a home and a business for its first owner, a Mr. Edward Smith, who operated a tavern on the first floor. Today it houses the offices of the Historic Annapolis Foundation.

4–5

Continue on Pinkney Street to Randall Street, where you will encounter the **Middleton Tavern**. This building was used around 1750 as an inn for seamen, but today it houses an excellent restaurant and oyster bar, a focal point of the waterfront. On sunny days, this is a busy place with crowds strolling, sightseeing, having picnics or enjoying the restaurants, bars and snack shops. There's plenty of seating around the head of the harbor, which is a popular place to watch boats from around the world come and go.

5–6

A few steps away, the Victualling Warehouse (77 Main Street) was used for the storage of food and supplies during the Revolutionary War. Today, as the **Museum Store**, it is operated by the Historic Annapolis

Streetside parking spaces anywhere near the waterfront are a rarity in the summer. Your best bet is the public parking garages on Rowe Boulevard, Calvert Street and South Street.

Foundation, an excellent place to learn about the historic renovations and archaeological digs taking place in and around Annapolis.

6–7

Follow Compromise Street, turning northwest on Duke of Gloucester Street. Charles Carroll was the only Catholic signer of the Declaration of Independence, and his magnificent house and garden at No. 107 are open to the public. The **Charles Carroll House** is often used for public events, including 18th-century teas, period musical concerts and historic programs.

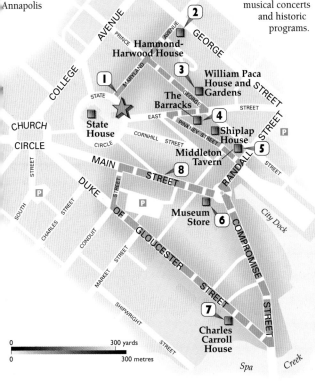

Along colorful Main Street you can buy anything from handblown glass to sushi

7–8

Continue up Duke of Gloucester Street, turning north on Conduit Street and then east on Main Street. Explore some of Annapolis's best and most interesting boutiques, shops and restaurants as you wend your way back down to **Annapolis Harbor**.

TAKING A BREAK

For fresh seafood try **O'Brien's Oyster Bar** (near the docks). **Yin Yankee Café** (105 Main Street) has good sushi.

Charles Carroll House
✉ 107 Duke of Gloucester Street
☎ 410/269-1737; ⏰ Sat 10–2, Sun noon–4; other times by appointment (tel: 410/269-1737); closed Nov–May 💲 Inexpensive

Hammond–Harwood House
✉ 19 Maryland Avenue
☎ 410/263-4683 ⏰ Apr–Oct Tue–Sun noon–4. Tours on the hour 💲 Inexpensive

Historic Annapolis Foundation Museum Store
✉ 77 Main Street ☎ 410/268-5576; www.annapolis.org ⏰ Apr–Dec Mon–Thu 10–6, Sun 11–6; Jan–Mar Tue–Sun 10–6 💲 Free

ANNAPOLIS: INSIDE INFO

Getting there Annapolis is approximately 30 miles (48km) east of Washington. **MTA** (tel: 410/539-5000) offers a Washington to Annapolis service every afternoon. Private carriers also offer services (Annapolis Bus Company: tel: 410/266-0602)

Top tip Water tours are a great way to see Annapolis. Watermark Tours (tel: 410/268-7600) offers a 40-minute tour of Spa Creek (including the Naval Academy) that gives an insight into the town and its history. The tours leave several times daily from the town waterfront.

Walks

1 WHITE HOUSE AND FEDERAL TRIANGLE

Walk

From the lavish art and architecture of the Federal Triangle to the elegant mansions and galleries surrounding the White House, this walk will take you through the heart of Washington, past and present. Much of the walk follows Pennsylvania Avenue, Washington's famous thoroughfare of presidential parades and festivities. Here you'll find some of Washington's most important government buildings, as well as a historic and still thriving theater district. Closer to the White House, you'll stroll past the mansions in an area that was once the city's first residential neighborhood.

1–2

Start at the intersection of Pennsylvania and Constitution avenues. Here, in a small triangular plaza, the **Andrew Mellon Memorial** commemorates the man who founded the

DISTANCE 1.25 miles (2km) **TIME** 1 hour, more if you visit attractions
START POINT Pennsylvania Avenue at Constitution Avenue ✚ 195 E3
END POINT Corcoran Gallery ✚ 194 B4

National Gallery of Art across the street. Walk up the south side of Pennsylvania Avenue, passing the **Federal Trade Commission Building** with its powerful statues and ornate stone carvings.

Cross 7th Street to the **National Archives** (restored and reopened in 2003, ▶ 68). Here you can step inside for a quick look at the original U.S. Constitution, the Declaration of Independence and the Bill of Rights, which are just three unique examples of the millions of historic documents stored here. Admission is free.

Preceding page: Elegant row houses in Georgetown

Right: A few of the historic homes near the White House

2–3

Return to 7th Street and cross Pennsylvania Avenue, continuing west along the north side of the street. Across from the National Archives is the quirky **Temperance Fountain**. In 1880 a dentist named Henry Cogswell gave the fountain to the city, so that

legendary law-enforcement organization started in 1908. The building is named after J. Edgar Hoover, who ran the organization with an iron hand from 1924 to 1973. Tours are available.

4–5

Turn north on 10th Street and walk one block to **Ford's Theatre** (▶ 69). It was here, on April 14, 1865, that President Abraham Lincoln was assassinated. Fully restored to its 1860s appearance, the theater stages classic American plays and contains a museum with exhibits on the assassination. Tours are available. Across the street is

Washingtonians would always have a nonalcoholic beverage at hand.

3–4

Continue west along Pennsylvania Avenue to the **FBI Building**. This nondescript 1970s-style glass and concrete box houses the

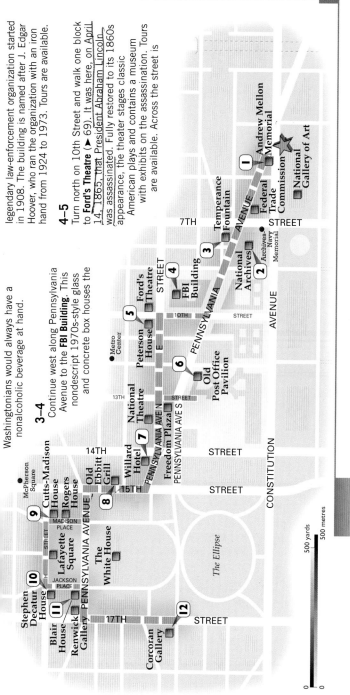

Taking a Break

The elegant **Old Ebbit Grill** (➤72) has been in continuous operation since 1865. Or there's contemporary Latin American cooking at Ceiba (➤71).

inauguration, had to be physically restrained by his staff as he attempted to sneak out of his room (where he was staying with his wife) to visit his mistress. But the Willard is best known as the place where lobbyists have come for decades to meet and shape the decisions of, politicians. Many such meetings took place in the hotel lobby, which led to the coining of the term "lobbyist."

7–8

Turn north on 15th Street and walk one block to the **Old Ebbit Grill** (➤72). In 1983, it moved into this building, a former vaudeville theater whose headliners included George Burns, Gracie Allen and the Barrymores.

8–9

Continue along 15th Street and you come to Pennsylvania Avenue again (Pennsylvania Avenue ceases to exist in front of the White House

Peterson House, where Lincoln was taken after being shot and where he died. Ironically, in 1865 Peterson House was a boarding house that rented rooms to (among others) Lincoln's assassin, actor John Wilkes Booth.

5–6

Walk back to E Street and turn right. E Street joins Pennsylvania Avenue across from Freedom Plaza. On the north side of the street is the historic **National Theatre**, which dates to 1835. On the night he was assassinated, Lincoln was originally scheduled to attend a performance here, but he changed his mind at the last moment, opting for Ford's Theatre instead. Across the street stands the **Old Post Office Pavilion**, a wondrously Romanesque building with a lofty clock tower, whose main courtyard is a Romanesque Revival mall with interesting shops and restaurants.

6–7

Continue along Pennsylvania Avenue, crossing 14th Street to the **Willard InterContinental Hotel**. The Willard (➤41) is perhaps Washington's most legendary hotel. It was here that Lincoln hid while waiting for his inauguration, as his staff feared for his life. It was also here that President Warren Harding, while awaiting his

At the Old Post Office Pavilion you can ride the elevator to the top of the clock tower for fabulous views

but starts again behind it). Turn west on Pennsylvania for a few paces, turning north on Madison Place.

The park to your left is **Lafayette Square**, filled with monuments to various heroes from American history. To your right are three historic row houses. No. 17, **Rogers House**, has a dark history. It was on the front steps that young Attorney General Phillip Barton Key II (son of national anthem writer Francis Scott Key) was shot to death by a jealous husband, Congressman Daniel Sickles – the first American to successfully use the temporary insanity plea to be acquitted of murder. It was also in this house, on the night of Lincoln's assassination, that one of John Wilkes Booth's co-conspirators unsuccessfully attempted to murder Lincoln's secretary of state. Two doors north, at 1520 H Street, stands the 1820 **Cutts-Madison House**, the famous salon of first lady Dolley Madison, where she entertained the crème de la crème of Washington's high society until her death in 1849.

9–10

Walk west along H Street. At 748 Jackson Place is the **Stephen Decatur House**, where that naval war hero lived with his beautiful wife Susan. Young, wealthy and famous, the

Lafayette Square looking onto the White House

Decaturs were the toast of Washington until Stephen was killed in a duel in 1820.

10–11

Continue along Jackson Place, turning west on Pennsylvania Avenue. **Blair House**, at No. 1650, is used as a guest house for

presidential visitors and has served on several occasions as a temporary White House – most notably in 1950, when the Trumans moved in during White House renovations.

In November of that year, a pair of Puerto Rican nationalists tried to assassinate the president by rushing Blair House with guns blazing. Secret Service agents returned fire, killing one of the attackers and badly wounding the other, but not before one of their own agents, Leslie Coffelt, was mortally wounded. A plaque outside the house commemorates the event.

Next door stands the elegant **Renwick Gallery** (▶ 115). Named for its designer, James Renwick, the building was originally created to house the Corcoran Gallery of Art's collection. Within a few years, however, the Corcoran outgrew it and relocated down the street. Today the gallery is operated by the Smithsonian and houses an exceptional collection of American artwork and crafts.

11–12

Walk south on 17th Street for two blocks to the **Corcoran Gallery of Art** (▶ 115). Built in 1897, this beautiful *beaux-arts* building has one of the most impressive private collections of European and American art in the world.

s

2 GEORGETOWN
Walk

DISTANCE 2.2 miles (3.5km) **TIME** 2–3 hours
START POINT Washington Harbour  196 C1
END POINT Wisconsin Avenue  196 C2

Like a skilled politician, Georgetown has many faces. There is historic Georgetown, with the C&O Canal and cobbled streets lined with 200-year-old row houses. There is collegiate Georgetown, bursting with the exuberance of its student population. And there is wealthy Georgetown, with its restored mansions and power cocktail parties. But the best Georgetown is discovered on foot, along shady streets with beautiful homes. Its vibrant boutiques, funky shops, lively restaurants and jumping nightspots can be found along M Street and Wisconsin Avenue.

1–2

The waterfront plaza at **Washington Harbour** is a fun place to stroll – enjoy the fountains and

Georgetown's busy downtown presents a cornucopia of

maybe take a short walk along the river-front boardwalk. When you're ready, cross K Street and head up Thomas Jefferson Street (crossing the C&O Canal), continuing to M Street. Across M Street and just west is the **Old Stone House** (▶118). Built by Pennsylvania cabinetmaker Christopher Layman in 1765, this is the oldest house in Washington, and has been a boarding house, a tavern, a craftsman's studio and a house of ill repute. It is said to be one of the most haunted houses in Washington.

2–3

Continue west along M Street, with its shops and restaurants. A block past Wisconsin Avenue you can't miss the **Shops at Georgetown Park** mall, on the south side of the street. Once the site of a huge tobacco warehouse, the mall is home to an eclectic group of shops, as well as a small **museum** that highlights the neighborhood's history. The building just west of the Shops at Georgetown Park mall, at No. 3276, is **Market House**. Built in 1865, it is one of the oldest open-air market buildings in Washington, and is now the premises of **Dean & DeLuca** (▶131), the ultimate yuppie grocer.

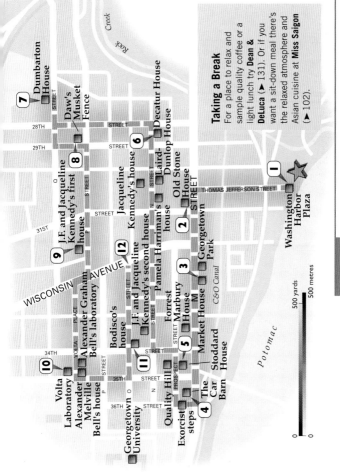

Taking a Break

For a place to relax and sample quality coffee or a light lunch try **Dean & DeLuca** (▶131). Or if you want a sit-down meal there's the relaxed atmosphere and Asian cuisine at **Miss Saigon** (▶102).

Georgetown's quiet side streets are lined with fine homes and gracious gardens

3–4

Cross to the north side of M Street and continue west to the **Forrest Marbury House** (3350 M Street), built in 1788. In 1791 George Washington met here with landowners to negotiate the land transfers that would create Washington, D.C. At M and 35th streets is the **Car Barn**, which from the late 1800s until 1950 was used to house the city's streetcars. Now full of offices, it has a 140-foot tall (42.5m) clock tower that once contained passenger elevators.

Continue to 36th Street and turn north, where you'll see the steep set of **steps** made famous in the 1973 movie *The Exorcist*.

4–5

Turn east along Prospect Street. This area once contained the homes of some of Washington's wealthiest residents. Two houses in particular are worth noting: **Quality Hill** at 3425 Prospect was built in 1798 and at 3400 Prospect Street is **Stoddard House,** which was built in 1787 by Benjamin Stoddard, the first secretary of the U.S. Navy.

5–6

Turn north on 34th Street, then east on N Street, which has been home to some of

Washington socialite and wife of statesman Averell Harriman. The **Laird-Dunlop House** (No. 3014) was built in 1799. Its most famous resident was Abraham Lincoln's son Robert, and it is currently owned by *The Washington Post's* former editor Ben Bradlee. Near the end of the street, No. 2812 was the modest **Decatur House** that Susan Decatur moved into when her husband, dashing naval war hero Stephen, was killed in a duel in 1820.

6–7

Turn north on 28th Street and walk four blocks north to Q Street. Just east of here along Q Street stand several of the area's most prominent homes, including **Dumbarton House** (▶ 118), which has been restored and is open to the public. Tradition has it that this house is where President James Madison and his wife rendezvoused when the British attacked Washington in 1814.

Georgetown's most famous residents. From 1957 until he became president in 1960, John F. Kennedy and his wife lived at **No. 3307.** Three blocks east at **No. 3038** was where Jacqueline Kennedy lived after Kennedy's assassination, and it was then the home of the late Pamela Harriman, renowned

7–8

Walk one block west on Q Street and then turn south on 29th Street. Continue one block to P Street, turn west again, and look for

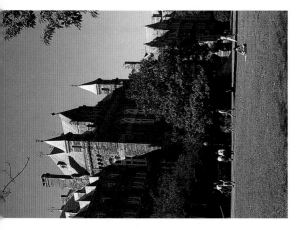

The ivy-covered walls of Georgetown University give it a distinguished air

Georgetown has an eye-pleasing style

considered his greatest life's work) at Volta Laboratory, founded by Bell and named for his laboratory.

10–11

Turn south onto 35th Street. On your right is Georgetown University. On your left, at No. 1527, is the **Alexander Melville Bell House**, the stately home bought by Alexander Graham Bell for his father. Continue south and turn east on O Street. A block farther along, look for No. 3322, the **Bodisco House**, which was home to Russian minister Baron de Bodisco in the 1830s. Bodisco liked America so much that he ended up staying here. He married an American and is buried in nearby Oak Hill Cemetery.

11–12

Continue along O Street to Wisconsin Avenue. Influenced by their proximity to Georgetown University, the shops and restaurants along Wisconsin have a younger and funkier flavor than their more mainstream cousins on nearby M Street.

the unusual wrought-iron fence fronting Nos. 2803 to 2811. Known as **Daw's Musket Fence**, it was built in the 1860s by an eccentric locksmith, Reuben Daw, out of musket barrels from the 1848 Mexican-American War.

8–9

Turn and walk west on P Street. Just past 31st Street, look for **No. 3271**. This is the first Georgetown house that John and Jacqueline Kennedy lived in; they purchased it in 1953.

9–10

Continue west along P Street, turning north on busy Wisconsin Avenue, then turning almost immediately west again on Volta Place. After you cross 34th Street look for **No. 3414**. This private home was once a simple carriage house, part of an estate bought by Scottish-born inventor Alexander Graham Bell for his father. The inventor, however, took over the carriage house as a laboratory, and here he worked on his disk-graphophone and many technological devices to aid the deaf. He named the lab the **Volta Laboratory** after a French prize he had earned. Farther along, at the corner of Volta Place and 35th Street, is the American Association for the Teaching of Speech to the Deaf (a pursuit that Bell

3 DUPONT CIRCLE AND EMBASSY ROW

Walk

DISTANCE 2 miles (3.2km) **TIME** 2 hours
START POINT Dupont Circle, southeast corner ✚ 197 F2
END POINT Connecticut Avenue ✚ 197 E3

This walk has the best of everything: lively city streets jam-packed with funky shops and great restaurants; quiet tree-lined avenues with magnificent mansions, a world-class art collection and enough historic sites and museums to keep anyone happy. What makes the Dupont Circle and Embassy Row area so fascinating is its collision of cultures. Here the world of diplomats and power lunch spots rubs elbows with the vibrant, arty Dupont Circle and the mega-wealthy enclave of stately homes along Kalorama Road and Wyoming Avenue.

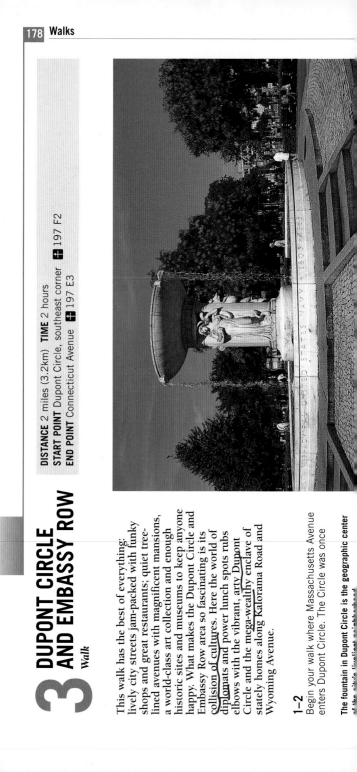

1–2

Begin your walk where Massachusetts Avenue enters Dupont Circle. The Circle was once

The fountain in Dupont Circle is the geographic center
of the city's liveliest neighborhood

Heurich Mansion at No. 1307. Built in 1894 for Washington's beer-brewing baron, Christian Heurich, the fully restored mansion is now owned by the Historical Society of Washington and is open for tours. Inside, the decor is wonderfully Teutonic and includes a *Bierstube* (beer room).

3–4

Walk back around Dupont Circle and continue north on New Hampshire Avenue, passing the **Slovenian Embassy** and turning west on Q Street by the **Argentine Embassy.**

Walk along Q Street to 21st Street, where a **statue of Mahatma Gandhi,** India's nationalist leader, creates a striking contrast to the ornate wealth of the buildings that surround him.

entirely surrounded by the homes of some of Washington's richest and most famous residents. The triangular lot between Massachusetts and Connecticut avenues was where Alexander Graham Bell's house once stood. The elegant mansion on the east side of Dupont Circle, between Massachusetts and New Hampshire avenues, was once owned by newspaper heiress Cissy Patterson and is now home to the elite **Washington Club,** which she founded. The long list of famous guests who have stayed here includes Charles Lindbergh and President Calvin Coolidge, who used it as a temporary White House during renovations to the original.

2–3

Proceed along the Circle to New Hampshire Avenue and walk south one block to the

Map labels

The Lindens
Embassy
CIRCLE
KALORAMA ROAD
WYOMING AVENUE
William Howard Taft's house
Warren G. Harding's house
CALIFORNIA
23RD STREET
Woodrow Wilson's house
CONNECTICUT AVENUE
PHELPS PLACE
S STREET
Textile Museum
Alice Pike Barney Studio House
MASSACHUSETTS AVENUE
SHERIDAN CIRCLE
Irish Embassy
Sudanese Embassy
Herbert Hoover's house
R STREET
21ST
Greek Embassy
FLORIDA AVENUE
Cosmos Club
Indian Embassy
Phillips Collection
Anderson House
Q STREET
Jockey Club
Gandhi statue
Walsh-McLean House
Argentine Embassy
NEW HAMPSHIRE AVE
Slovenian Embassy
Washington Club
DUPONT CIRCLE
Dupont Circle
Heurich Mansion
NEW AVENUE
P STREET
Rock Creek

9
10
7
8
6
5
4
2
1
3

0   500 yards
0   500 metres

The cafés on Dupont Circle provide a welcome rest from the busy street scene

To the north of this intersection is the **Phillips Collection** (➤ 122), which houses one of the city's most impressive private collections of art. Next to the Phillips Collection is a lovely mansion that now serves as the **Indian Embassy**. Beyond that, on Massachusetts Avenue, is another of Washington's exclusive private clubs, the **Cosmos Club**. Looking south you'll see a tall, ornate mansion on the southeast corner of 21st Street and Massachusetts Avenue, the **Walsh-McLean House**. This elegant mansion was built in 1901 in a *beaux-arts* style by Thomas Walsh, who made his money in the gold fields of Colorado (and whose daughter, Evalyn, was the last private owner of the Hope Diamond). The house is now the site of the Indonesian Embassy. Across 21st Street is a legendary power eatery, the **Jockey Club**.

4–5
Strolling northwest along Massachusetts Avenue, you'll pass the splendid mansion known as **Anderson House** at No. 2118. Built in 1902 by wealthy diplomat Lars Anderson, the house is now the headquarters of the

first-born male descendants of George Washington's Revolutionary War officers. A stunning example of *beaux-arts* architecture, the house contains many fine artwork from

Europe, Asia and America, as well as exhibits of Revolutionary War-era military memorabilia. Continuing along Massachusetts, you'll pass several embassies between 22nd Street and Sheridan Circle, including Luxembourg (No. 2200), Turkey (No. 2202), Sudan (No. 2210), Bahamas (No. 2220), Turkmenistan (No. 2207), Greece (No. 2211), Egypt (No. 2232) and Ireland (No. 2234).

5–6
Follow Massachusetts around Sheridan Circle. On the east side of the Circle at No. 2306 is the **Alice Pike Barney Studio House**. Built in 1902, it was the home of American painter and playwright Alice Pike Barney.

In addition to being her studio, it was also where she entertained many of the creative luminaries of her time, including French actors Sarah Bernhardt, tenor Enrico Caruso the Barrymore acting family and artist James McNeill Whistler.

6–7

Continue along Massachusetts, turning east on S Street. There are several interesting houses on this block, including **Woodrow Wilson House** at No. 2340. Wilson and his wife moved to the house in 1921, and he passed away here in 1924. The house is now open to the public as a museum dedicated to the president's life and works. Next door you can explore the **Textile Museum**, which began as an exhibit of Oriental rugs collected by George Hewitt Myers in 1925. Today the collection contains more than 14,000 items, with textiles and rugs from virtually every corner of the globe, some dating back 3,000 years. Also of interest on this block is the **Herbert Hoover House** at 2300 S Street, where he lived before and after his presidency. Today it houses the Embassy of Myanmar (Burma).

7–8

Turn north on Phelps Place. Walk two blocks to California Street, turn west and then north along 23rd Street. The large house on the corner of Wyoming Avenue and 23rd Street, **William Taft House,** was Taft's home when he

served as Chief Justice of the Supreme Court (the only past president to hold this office) until his death in 1930. Today the house is part of the United Arab Republic Embassy. A few paces farther, turn west on Wyoming Avenue and proceed to the **Warren G. Harding House** at 2314 Wyoming, the modest house where the Ohio senator lived before he became the 29th president in 1921.

Taking a Break

Two good spots are **La Tomate** (➤ 128) for Italian specialties, or Tex-Mex at **Lauriol Plaza** (➤ 126).

Places To Visit

Anderson House

✉ 2118 Massachusetts Avenue ☎ 202/785-2040 ⊙ Self-guiding tours: Tue–Sat 1–4

Woodrow Wilson House

✉ 2340 S Street ☎ 202/387-4062 ⊙ Tue–Sun 10–4; closed major hols

Textile Museum

✉ 2320 S Street ☎ 202/667-0441 ⊙ Mon–Sat 10–5, Sun 1–5; closed major hols

President Woodrow Wilson's home on S Street is now a museum open to the public

8–9

Continue west along Wyoming Avenue, turning right on Kalorama Road. The homes along Kalorama constitute what is perhaps Washington's most elite community. A "modest" home here – on this street that is anything but – was recently listed for a cool $4.6 million.

About halfway along Kalorama, at No. 2401, is **The Lindens**, a graceful wood-frame structure whose traditional New England lines seem a bit out of character with the neighboring architecture. Hardly surprising, since the house was actually built in Danvers, Massachusetts, in 1754 and relocated to this site in 1935.

Continue to follow the loop of Kalorama Circle, which takes you past more beautiful homes and returns to Kalorama Road. Then head west on Kalorama to see the massive estate at No. 2221 built in 1807 for Joel Barlow, one-time ambassador to France.

This is the **Hayes-Hammond House**, best known as the estate of wealthy mining magnate John Hayes Hammond (1855–1936). Hammond became friends with many of the influential politicians, prominent scientists and creative glitterati

of his day. Regular guests in this house included Samuel Clemens (Mark Twain), Alexander Graham Bell, Wilbur and Orville Wright, Gugliemo Marconi, William Howard Taft and Scottish-born philanthropist Andrew Carnegie. For the past 30 years the building has served as part of the French Embassy.

9–10

A block beyond the French Embassy, turn south on Connecticut Avenue. Between here and Dupont Circle lies one of D.C.'s best shopping districts. The boutiques, galleries, bookstores and restaurants along this route should keep you busy for the rest of the day.

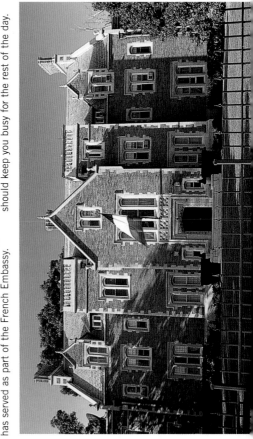

This mansion on Kalorama Road was home to a mining magnate but is now the French embassor's residence

Practicalities

GETTING ADVANCE INFORMATION

Websites
- Washington D.C. Convention and Tourism Corporation: www.washington.org
- The Smithsonian museums: www.si.edu

In the U.S.
Washington D.C. Convention and Tourism Corporation, 901 7th Street, Washington, D.C. 20001-3719
☎ 202/789-7000

In the U.K.
24 Grosvenor Square London W1A 1AE
☎ 0904 245 0100
www.usembassy.org.uk

BEFORE YOU GO

WHAT YOU NEED

	U.K.	Germany	U.S.A.	Canada	Australia	Ireland	Netherlands	Spain
● Required ○ Suggested ▲ Not required — Some countries require a passport to remain valid for a minimum period (usually at least six months) beyond the date of entry – check before you travel.								
Passport/National Identity Card	●	●	▲	●	●	●	●	●
Visa (regulations can change – check before you travel)	▲	▲	▲	▲	▲	▲	▲	▲
Onward or Return Ticket	●	●	▲	▲	●	●	●	●
Health Inoculations (tetanus and polio)	▲	▲	▲	▲	▲	▲	▲	▲
Health Documentation (► 188, Health)	▲	▲	▲	▲	▲	▲	▲	▲
Travel Insurance	●	●	▲	○	●	●	●	●
Driver's License (state or national) ✓	●	●	●	●	●	●	●	●
Car Insurance Certificate ✓	n/a	n/a	●	●	n/a	n/a	n/a	n/a
Car Registration Document ✓	n/a	n/a	●	●	n/a	n/a	n/a	n/a

WHEN TO GO

Washington

☐ Peak season ☐ Low season

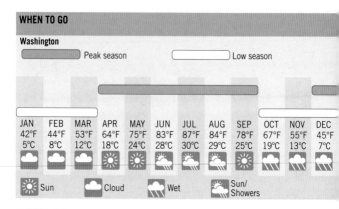

JAN	FEB	MAR	APR	MAY	JUN	JUL	AUG	SEP	OCT	NOV	DEC
42°F	44°F	53°F	64°F	75°F	83°F	87°F	84°F	78°F	67°F	55°F	45°F
5°C	8°C	12°C	18°C	24°C	28°C	30°C	29°C	25°C	19°C	13°C	7°C

☀ Sun ☁ Cloud ☂ Wet ⛅ Sun/Showers

Temperatures are the **average daily maximum** for each month. Average daily minimum temperatures are approximately 15 to 20 degrees lower.
The best times of year for good weather are April, May and early June, as well as September and early October. In July and August the temperature often rises to 90°F (32°C), and humidity tends to be high.
Significant snowfall rarely occurs before Christmas. However, most years there are usually three or four snowfalls of 6 inches (15cm) or less, with rare heavy snowfalls of as much as 18 inches (45.5cm). Snowfall of any amount can disrupt life in the city and create a traffic nightmare. But winter temperatures are usually fairly mild and most snowfalls will usually melt away within a few days.

In Canada
The Embassy of the
United States of America
490 Sussex Drive
Ottawa, Ontario K1N 1G8
☎ (900) 451-2778
http://ottawa.usembassy.gov

In Australia
U.S. Embassy Canberra
Moonah Place
Yarralumla ACT 2600
☎ (02) 6214 5600

http://usembassy-australia.state.gov

GETTING THERE

By Air Washington has three main airports: **Ronald Reagan Washington National** (DCA; www.metwashairports.com/reagan), **Washington Dulles International** (IAD; www.metwashairports.com/dulles) and **Baltimore-Washington International** (BWI; www.bwiairport.com). Ronald Reagan Washington National Airport is serviced primarily by domestic carriers within a 1,500-mile (2,145km) limit. Baltimore-Washington International receives a number of international flights. Washington Dulles International receives many international flights, including direct flights from cities in Europe, Africa and Asia. **Air fares** tend to cost most in summer, and at Easter and Christmas. Springtime Cherry Blossom Festival packages are often available at special prices. Check with airlines, travel agents, flight brokers, travel sections in newspapers or the internet for deals. Nondirect flights may offer savings. Tickets for short stays are can be expensive, unless a Saturday night is included. **Approximate flying times to Washington**: east coast of Australia (22 hours), New Zealand (20 hours), Berlin (9 hours), London and Dublin (7 hours), Vancouver (6 hours), Montreal (2 hours), Toronto (2.5 hours). All airport **taxes** are usually included in your ticket price.

By Rail and Bus Alternative options for travelers from the U.S. or Canada include **Amtrak** (tel: 800/872-7245). High-speed trains include the Amtrak Acela, which runs direct from Boston and New York to Washington (from New York to Washington takes 2.5 hours). High-speed train fares are comparable to air fares but offer the advantage of traveling from city center to city center. Trains arrive at Union Station. The **Greyhound Bus Station** is near Union Station at 1005 1st Street N.E. (tel: 202/289-5160, toll free: 800/231-2222).

TIME

L Washington is on Eastern Standard Time (EST), five hours behind Greenwich meantime (GMT -5). Daylight savings time (GMT -4) is in effect from early April (when clocks are advanced one hour) to late October.

CURRENCY AND FOREIGN EXCHANGE

Currency The basic unit of currency in the United States is the dollar ($1). One dollar is 100 cents. **Bills** (notes) come in denominations of $1, $5, $10, $20, $50 and $100. All notes are green and are the same size, so look carefully at the amount on them. **Coins** come in denominations of 1 cent (penny), 5 cents (nickel), 10 cents (dime), 25 cents (quarter) and 50 cents (half-dollar). There are also one-dollar coins, but these are comparatively rare.
An **unlimited amount** of U.S. dollars can be imported or exported.
U.S. dollar **traveler's checks** are the best way to carry money, and they are accepted as cash in most places (not taxis), as are **credit cards** (Amex, VISA, MasterCard, Diners Club).

Exchange The best place to exchange foreign currency for U.S. currency is at a bank. If you need to exchange currency outside business hours, try a major hotel or Thomas Cook Currency Exchange at either the Shops at Georgetown Park mall (tel: 202/872-1233) or Union Station (tel: 202/371-9219). Automated teller cards can usually be used to withdraw money from your bank account in U.S. currency.

TIME DIFFERENCES

GMT	Washington	U.S.A. (Los Angeles)	U.K.	Germany	Australia
12 noon	← 7am	← 4am	12 noon	→ 1pm	→ 10pm

CLOTHING SIZES

U.K.	Rest of Europe	U.S.A.	
36	46	36	
38	48	38	
40	50	40	
42	52	42	Suits
44	54	44	
46	56	46	
7	41	8	
7.5	42	8.5	
8.5	43	9.5	
9.5	44	10.5	Shoes
10.5	45	11.5	
11	46	12	
14.5	37	14.5	
15	38	15	
15.5	39/40	15.5	
16	41	16	Shirts
16.5	42	16.5	
17	43	17	
8	34	6	
10	36	8	
12	38	10	
14	40	12	Dresses
16	42	14	
18	44	16	
4.5	38	6	
5	38	6.5	
5.5	39	7	
6	39	7.5	Shoes
6.5	40	8	
7	41	8.5	

NATIONAL HOLIDAYS

Jan 1	New Year's Day
Third Mon Jan	Martin Luther King, Jr. Day
Third Mon Feb	Presidents' Day
Mar/Apr	Good Friday (half day)
	Easter Monday (whole day)
Last Mon May	Memorial Day
Jul 4	Independence Day
First Mon Sep	Labor Day
Second Mon Oct	Columbus Day
Nov 11	Veterans' Day
Fourth Thu Nov	Thanksgiving
Dec 25	Christmas Day

Some stores open on national holidays.

OPENING HOURS

○ Stores ● Offices ● Banks ● Post Offices ● Museums/Monuments ● Pharmacies

8am 9am 10am noon 1pm 2pm 4pm 5pm 7pm

☐ Day ☐ Midday ☐ Evening

Stores Hours vary greatly, but most open until 9pm on one day. Some open Sun noon–5.

Banks Some open until 3pm, or Fri until 6pm. Most are closed Sat, all are closed Sun.

Post Offices Open until 1pm Sat. Smaller post offices keep shorter hours.

Museums Hours vary. Most open 9:30 or 10 to 5 or 6. Some stay open longer hours Thu, Fri or Sat. Most are closed Mon. All Smithsonian museums (except the zoo) open at 10 and close at 5:30.

Places of Worship Washington has many churches, synagogues, mosques, etc. See *Yellow Pages* for details.

PERSONAL SAFETY

Violent crime in Washington has fallen sharply in recent years, but it is still wise to take sensible precautions.

- Carry only the cash you need; keep other cash/ valuables in the hotel safe.
- Don't walk alone in the Mall in the early evening, and avoid quiet areas after 10pm
- The areas northeast and southeast of the Capitol, and south of I-395, are some of the least desirable neighborhoods. Do not walk in these areas.
- Report theft or mugging to the police (required for an insurance claim).

Emergency Assistance:
☎ 911 from any phone

ELECTRICITY

The power supply is 110/120 volts AC (60 cycles). Sockets take two-prong, flat-pin plugs.

An adaptor is needed for any appliances that have two-round-pin and three-pin plugs. European appliances need a voltage transformer.

TELEPHONES

calling. You'll need at least $5.50 in quarters for an overseas call. Some phones take prepaid phonecards (from drugstores and newsstands), some take credit cards. Dial 1 plus the area code for numbers within the U.S. and Canada. Dial 411 to find U.S. and Canadian numbers.

There are pay-phones on some street corners. Most are coin-operated. From public phones dial 0 for the operator and give the country, city and number you're

International Dialing Codes
Dial 011 followed by

U.K.:	44
Ireland:	353
Australia:	61
Germany:	49
The Netherlands:	31
Spain:	34

MAIL

Main post office: 2 Massachusetts Avenue, daily 7am–8pm (Mon–Fri 8pm–midnight). Handy mail boxes are on Constitution Avenue at 11th, 14th and 21st streets; Independence Avenue at 14th Street; and 15th Street at the Bureau of Engraving and Printing.

TIPS/GRATUITIES

Tipping is expected for all services. As a general guide the following applies:

Restaurants (service not included)	15–20%
Bar service	15%
Tour guides	Discretion
Hairdressers	15%
Taxis	15%
Chambermaids	$1 per day
Porters	$1 per bag

U.K.
☎ 202/588-7800

Ireland
☎ 202/462-3939

Canada
☎ 202/682-1740

Australia
☎ 202/797-3000

New Zealand
☎ 202/328-4800

HEALTH

Insurance Coverage of at least $1 million is strongly recommended; medical fees in the United States are unregulated. If you are involved in an accident in Washington you will be cared for by medical services and charged later.

Dental Services Your medical insurance coverage should include dental treatment, which is readily available but expensive. Most dentists accept credit cards, but some prefer cash or traveler's checks.

Weather Washington is very hot and humid in summer, particularly in July and August, when the sun can shine brightly for long periods. If you are out sightseeing, use a good sunscreen, cover up and drink plenty of fluids.

Drugs Pharmacies dispensing prescription and over-the-counter treatments can be found on many streets. If you need regular medication, bring your own drugs from home, along with the prescription (for U.S. Customs). CVS Pharmacy operates 24-hour pharmacies at 14th Street and 6 Dupont Circle, N.W. (tel: 202/785-1466).

Safe Water Drinking unboiled water is safe. Bottled mineral water is cheap and readily available.

CONCESSIONS

Students Holders of an International Student Identity Card are entitled to discounts on many attractions.
Senior Citizens On services and attractions, request a discount up-front. You may need to show proof of qualifying age (varies from 55 to 65).
Admission Charges Many attractions throughout the city, including all Smithsonian museums, the National Gallery of Art and all public monuments, are open to the public free of charge.
Metro A special unlimited-use, one-day pass is available for $5 from any Metro card machine.

TRAVELING WITH A DISABILITY

For an excellent **brochure,** contact Access Information at 301/528-8664 or www.disabilityguide.org. Most **monuments and memorials** have parking facilities and elevators. Some have sign-language interpreters. **Smithsonian museums** (tel: 202/633-2921) are wheelchair-accessible, and offer (with notice) sign-language interpreters and Braille or cassette materials. **Metro** stations offer reduced fares, priority seating and elevators; trains accommodate wheelchairs. Some buses have wheelchair lifts. For details, tel: 202/637-7000.

CHILDREN

In child-friendly Washington, baby-changing facilities are widely available. Children's events are listed in the Weekend section of *The Washington Post.*

RESTROOMS

It's best to use those in large hotels and stores, chain bookstores, galleries and museums.

CUSTOMS

The importation of wildlife souvenirs created from rare or endangered species may be either illegal or require a permit. Check your country's regulations before buying.

U.S. PRESIDENTS

President	Party	Term
George Washington	Federalist	1789–1796
John Adams	Federalist	1796–1800
Thomas Jefferson	Democratic-Republican	1800–1808
James Madison	Democratic-Republican	1808–1816
James Monroe	Democratic-Republican	1816–1824
John Quincy Adams	Democratic-Republican	1824–1828
Andrew Jackson	Democrat	1828–1836
Martin van Buren	Democrat	1836–1840
William H. Harrison	Whig	1840 (died in office)
John Tyler	Whig	1841–1844
James K. Polk	Democrat	1844–1848
Zachary Taylor	Whig	1848–1850 (died in office)
Millard Fillmore	Whig	1850–1852
Franklin Pierce	Democrat	1852–1856
James Buchanan	Democrat	1856–1860
Abraham Lincoln	Republican	1860–1865 (assassinated)
Andrew Johnson	Democrat	1865–1868
Ulysses S. Grant	Republican	1868–1876
Rutherford B. Hayes	Republican	1876–1880
James A. Garfield	Republican	1880–1881 (assassinated)
Chester A. Arthur	Republican	1881–1884
Grover Cleveland	Democrat	1884–1888
Benjamin Harrison	Republican	1888–1892
Grover Cleveland	Democrat	1892–1896
William McKinley	Republican	1896–1901 (assassinated)
Theodore Roosevelt	Republican	1901–1908
William Howard Taft	Republican	1908–1912
Woodrow Wilson	Democrat	1912–1920
Warren G. Harding	Republican	1920–1923 (died in office)
Calvin Coolidge	Republican	1923–1928
Herbert Hoover	Republican	1928–1932
Franklin D. Roosevelt	Democrat	1932–1945 (died in office)
Harry S. Truman	Democrat	1945–1952
Dwight D. Eisenhower	Republican	1952–1960
John F. Kennedy	Democrat	1960–1963 (assassinated)
Lyndon B. Johnson	Democrat	1963–1968
Richard M. Nixon	Republican	1968–1974 (resigned)
Gerald R. Ford	Republican	1974–1976
James Earl Carter	Democrat	1976–1980
Ronald Reagan	Republican	1980–1988
George Bush	Republican	1988–1992
Bill Clinton	Democrat	1992–2000
George W. Bush	Republican	2000–

CALENDAR OF EVENTS

Washington has many major festivals, parades and annual events. Contact the Washington D.C. Convention and Tourism Corporation, 9901 7th Street, 4th floor, Washington, D.C/ 20001-3719, tel: 202/789-7000 for details. Individual dates may change so call before making plans.

JANUARY
Third Monday – Martin Luther King, Jr.'s Birthday: Laying of wreaths at Lincoln Memorial; reading of the "I Have a Dream" speech and concerts.

FEBRUARY
Dates vary – Chinese New Year Parade: Dragon dancers, parades and fireworks in Chinatown.
12th – Abraham Lincoln's Birthday: Reading of the Gettysburg Address and laying of wreaths at the Lincoln Memorial.

MARCH
Around the 17th – St. Patrick's Day Festival: Parades along Constitution Avenue N.W. and festivities in Old Town Alexandria and Arlington House at Arlington Cemetery.
Mid to late March – Environmental Film Festival: Over 100 documentary, feature, children's and animated films, mostly free. Various venues.
End of month – Smithsonian Kite Flying Festival: Competitions open to all at the Washington Monument.

APRIL
Early April – National Cherry Blossom Festival: The famous cherry trees around the Tidal Basin near the Washington Monument are in bloom in late March/early April. A huge parade takes place along Constitution Avenue N.W., during which the festival queen is crowned. Also dancing, free concerts and races.
Easter Sun – Easter Sunrise Service: Memorial service at Arlington National Cemetery.

MAY
First weekend – Washington National Cathedral Flower Mart: flowers, entertainment for the kids and fantastic displays at the Cathedral.

Last Monday – Memorial Day: Services and speeches at the Arlington Cemetery, Vietnam Veterans Memorial and U.S. Navy Memorial. The National Symphony Orchestra performs at the Capitol.

JUNE
Last week June/first week July – Smithsonian Festival of American Folklife: Music, crafts and heritage events take place all along the Mall.

JULY
4th – Independence Day: Declaration of Independence read at the National Archives; parade along Constitution Avenue; a performance by the National Symphony Orchestra on the west steps of the Capitol. The day ends with a fireworks display.

AUGUST
Early August – Restaurant Week: Nearly 100 of the top restaurants offer fixed-price menus showcasing some of their signature dishes.

SEPTEMBER
Sunday before Labor Day – Labor Day Weekend Concert: the National Symphony Orchestra plays at the Capitol.
First Sunday after Labor Day – Adams-Morgan Day: a great fun neighborhood festival with music, crafts and food along 18th Street N.W.
Date varies – Black Family Reunion: Festival on the Mall to celebrate African-Americans.

OCTOBER
Date varies – Taste of Georgetown: Wisconsin Avenue N.W. hosts restaurant tastings, arts, crafts and children's entertainment.

NOVEMBER
11th – Veterans' Day Ceremonies: Services at 11am at Arlington Cemetery (the President is usually in attendance), Vietnam Veterans Memorial and U.S. Navy Memorial.

DECEMBER
Beginning of month – Christmas Tree Lightings: ceremonies to light the National (by the President) and Capitol Christmas trees.

Atlas

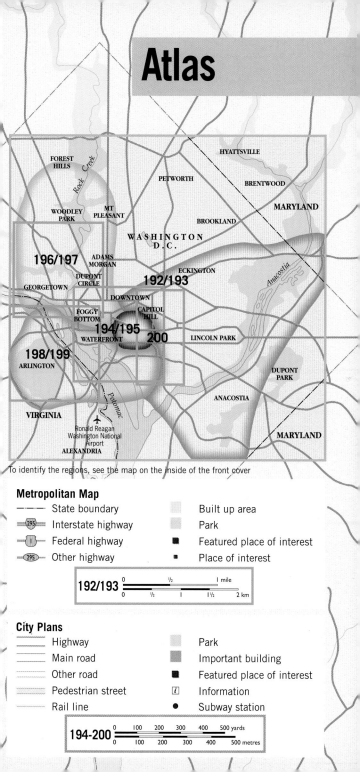

FOREST HILLS

Rock Creek

HYATTSVILLE

PETWORTH

BRENTWOOD

WOODLEY PARK

MT PLEASANT

MARYLAND

BROOKLAND

WASHINGTON D.C.

196/197

ADAMS MORGAN

ECKINGTON

Anacostia

DUPONT CIRCLE

GEORGETOWN

192/193

DOWNTOWN

FOGGY BOTTOM

CAPITOL HILL

194/195

200

WATERFRONT

LINCOLN PARK

198/199

ARLINGTON

DUPONT PARK

VIRGINIA

ANACOSTIA

Potomac

Ronald Reagan Washington National Airport

MARYLAND

ALEXANDRIA

To identify the regions, see the map on the inside of the front cover

Metropolitan Map

- –·–·–·– State boundary
- 295 Interstate highway
- 1 Federal highway
- 295 Other highway
- Built up area
- Park
- ■ Featured place of interest
- ▪ Place of interest

192/193

| 0 | ½ | 1 mile |
| 0 | ½ | 1 | 1½ | 2 km |

City Plans

- Highway
- Main road
- Other road
- Pedestrian street
- Rail line
- Park
- Important building
- ■ Featured place of interest
- [i] Information
- ● Subway station

194-200

| 0 | 100 | 200 | 300 | 400 | 500 yards |
| 0 | 100 | 200 | 300 | 400 | 500 metres |

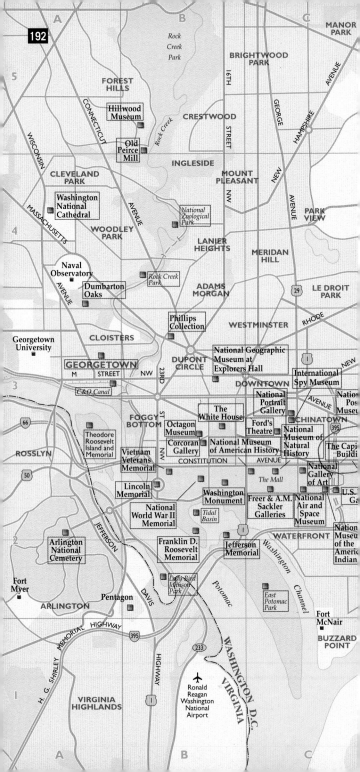

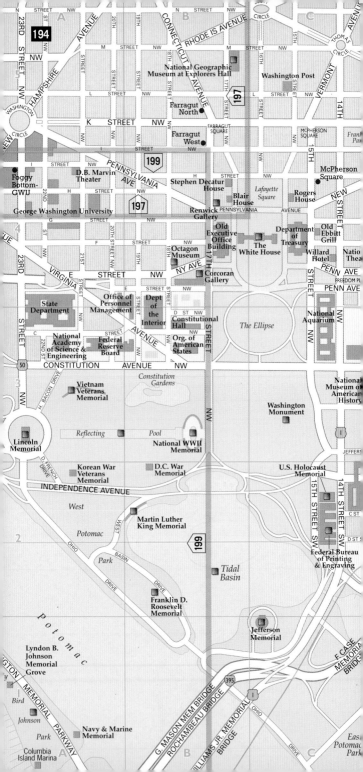

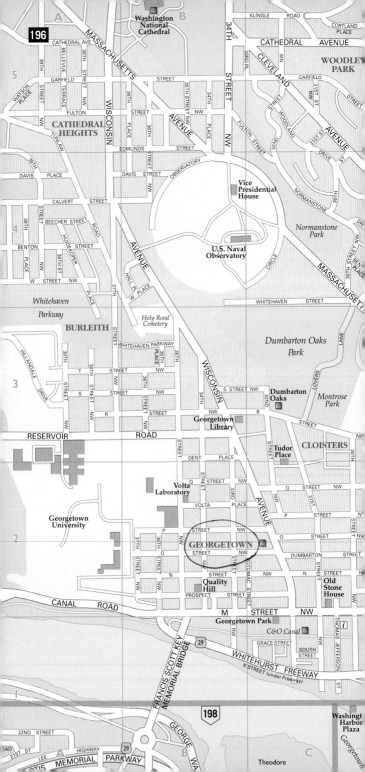

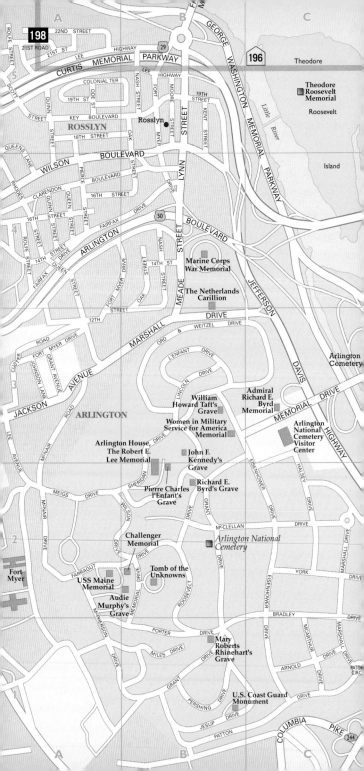

A   B   C

196

22ND STREET

21ST ROAD

21ST ST

LEE

21ST STREET

CURTIS   MEMORIAL   HIGHWAY

COLONIAL TER

PARKWAY

GEORGE

Theodore

Theodore
Roosevelt
Memorial

Roosevelt

ROLFE STREET

SCOTT STREET

QUINN STREET

19TH STREET

ODE ST

KEY BOULEVARD

NASH STREET

FORT STREET

MOORE STREET

19TH STREET

KENT STREET

WASHINGTON

Little River

Island

ROSSLYN

18TH STREET

OAK STREET

MYER

Rosslyn

LYNN

STREET

QUEENS LANE

RHODES STREET

WILSON

PIERCE STREET

CLARENDON

QUEEN STREET

QUINN STREET

BOULEVARD

16TH STREET

16TH STREET

STREET

BOULEVARD

DRIVE

MEMORIAL

PARKWAY

16TH STREET

ROLFE STREET

14TH STREET

FAIRFAX

QUEEN STREET

ARLINGTON

NASH STREET

OAK STREET

FORT MYER DRIVE

DRIVE

50

14TH STREET

MEADE

STREET

BOULEVARD

JEFFERSON

12TH STREET

STREET

Marine Corps
War Memorial

The Netherlands
Carillon

DAVIS

Arlington
Cemetery

Road

FORT MYER DRIVE

GRANT AVENUE

JOHNSON LANE

CLUSTER

AVENUE

MARSHALL

ORD

WEITZEL

DRIVE

&

DRIVE

L'ENFANT

DRIVE

JACKSON

ROAD

MCNAIR

LEE AVENUE

ARLINGTON

LINCOLN

DRIVE

William
Howard Taft's
Grave

Women in Military
Service for America
Memorial

Admiral
Richard E.
Byrd
Memorial

MEMORIAL

HIGHWAY

Arlington
National
Cemetery
Visitor
Center

HALSEY DRIVE

MEIGS

DRIVE

SHERIDAN

DRIVE

Arlington House,
The Robert E.
Lee Memorial

John F.
Kennedy's
Grave

Pierre Charles
l'Enfant's
Grave

Richard E.
Byrd's Grave

EISENHOWER

GRANT DRIVE

Fort
Myer

MCNAIR DRIVE

WILSON DRIVE

FARRAGUT DRIVE

Challenger
Memorial

DRIVE

MCCLELLAN

*Arlington National
Cemetery*

YORK

MARSHALL DRIVE

USS Maine
Memorial

Audie
Murphy's
Grave

MCPHERSON

PORTER

Tomb of the
Unknowns

ROOSEVELT

DRIVE

BRADLEY

EISENHOWER

MCARTHUR DRIVE

MARSHALL DRIVE

MILES DRIVE

Mary
Roberts
Rhinehart's
Grave

DRIVE

ARNOLD

PATTO
CIRC

GRANT DRIVE

PERSHING DRIVE

U.S. Coast Guard
Monument

DRIVE

JESUP DRIVE

PATTON

COLUMBIA

PIKE

244

A   B   C

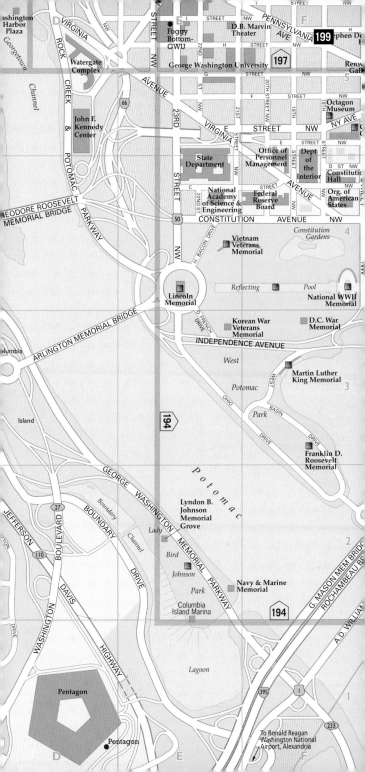

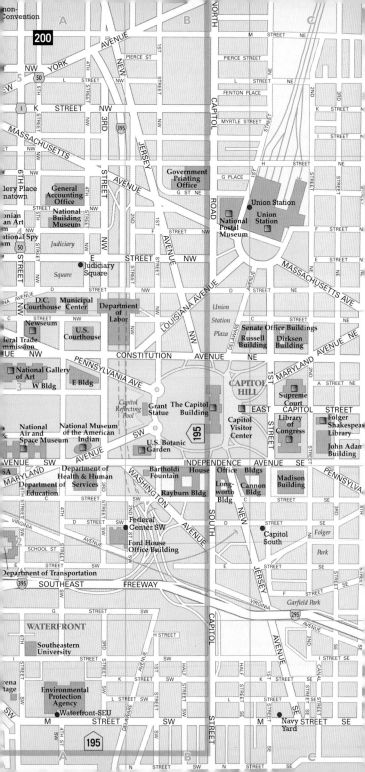

STREETPLAN INDEX

Picture credits

All front cover, back cover and spine images: AA Photo Library/Clive Sawyer.

The Automobile Association wishes to thank the following photographers, libraries and associations for their assistance with the preparation of this book.

ANNAPOLIS & ANNE ARUNDEL COUNTY CONFERENCE & VISITORS BUREAU 165, 168; BRIDGEMAN ART LIBRARY, LONDON 54/5 National Gallery of Art Washington D. C. USA, 55 National Gallery of Art, Washington D. C. USA, 58 National Gallery of Art, Washington D. C USA; BRUCE COLEMAN COLLECTION 13; CORBIS UK LTD 3(iii) Joseph Sohm; Chromosohm Inc., 3(iv) James P. Blair, 12/3 Catherine Karnow, 19 H. David Seawell, 61 James L. Amos, 98 Joseph Sohm; Chromosohm Inc., 109t Kelly-Mooney Photography, 118 Bob Rowan; Progressive Image, 137 James P. Blair, 148/9 Kelly-Mooney Photography, 150b Kelly-Mooney Photography, 153 Lee Snider, 161 Joseph Sohm; Chromosohm Inc., 164 Lee Snider, 169 James P. Blair, 174 Catherine Karnow, 176 James P. Blair, 177r Karen Huntt H. Mason, 181 Lee Snider; THE CORCORAN GALLERY OF ART 115, gift of Mrs Albert Bierstadt; JAMES DAVIS WORLDWIDE 52b; DUMBARTON OAKS 11, 11 inset, 123; MARY EVANS PICTURE LIBRARY 10t, 26, 111t; FREER GALLERY OF ART 66 photo by John Tsantes and Jeffrey Crespi; GETTYONE/STONE 18/9 b/g, 18, 173; ROBERT HARDING PICTURE LIBRARY 60, 65, 93, 94t; HULTON GETTY 14, 15, 16t, 16b, 17t, 20/1, 21, 25, 27, 31l, 111b, 146; COURTESY OF THE INTERNATIONAL SPY MUSEUM 32, 39; CATHERINE KARNOW 7, 8, 9b, 30, 99, 122, 142, 170, 182; NATIONAL AIR AND SPACE MUSEUM/ERIC LONG, SMITHSONIAN INSTITUTE 48t, 51b; THE NATIONAL ARBORETUM 149, 150t; THE NATIONAL GALLERY OF ART, WASHINGTON, D.C 56/7 Sir Peter Paul Rubens, Daniel in the Lions' Den, Ailsa Mellon Bruce Fund, Photograph © 2001 Board of Trustees, National Gallery of Art, Washington; NATIONAL MUSEUM OF AMERICAN HISTORY 49t, 63t, 62/3, 64; THE NATIONAL MUSEUM OF WOMEN IN THE ARTS 121; PETER NEWARK'S AMERICAN PICTURES 24/5 b/g and 26/7 b/g; NEWSEUM 70; THE PHILLIPS COLLECTION 108; PICTURES COLOUR LIBRARY 166; LARRY PORGES 191t, 191br; REX FEATURES LTD 10b, 17b, 85b, 91t; SMITHSONIAN'S NATIONAL ZOO/JESSIE COHEN 106, 109b, 120t, 120b; TOPHAM PICTUREPOINT 22 (Imageworks), 23t (Imageworks), 23b; TRIP PHOTO LIBRARY 59; UNITED STATES BOTANIC GARDEN 144; THE WHITE HOUSE COLLECTION, COURTESY THE WHITE HOUSE HISTORICAL ASSOCIATION 9t, 112t, 112b, 113, 114; WOLF TRAP, FILENE CENTER 28/9b photo by Scott Suchman

The remaining photographs are held in the Association's own photo library (AA PHOTO LIBRARY) and were taken by CLIVE SAWYER with the exception of the following: 2 (iii), 12, 31r, 45, 46, 48b, 50, 51t, 52/3, 68, 94b, 100, 110, 119, 124, 134, 143t, 143c, 143b, 155, 172, these were taken by ETHEL DAVIS.

Abbreviations for terms appearing above (t) top; (b) bottom; (l) left; (r) right; (c) centre

SPIRAL GUIDES

Questionnaire

Dear Traveler

Your comments, opinions and recommendations are very important to us. So please help us to improve our travel guides by taking a few minutes to complete this simple questionnaire.

Send to: Spiral Guides, MailStop 66, 1000 AAA Drive, Heathrow, FL 32746–5063

Your recommendations...

We always encourage readers' recommendations for restaurants, nightlife or shopping – if your recommendation is added to the next edition of the guide, we will send you a FREE AAA Spiral Guide of your choice. Please state below the establishment name, location and your reasons for recommending it.

_____

_____

_____

_____

_____

Please send me AAA Spiral_____

(see list of titles inside the back cover)

About this guide...

Which title did you buy?

_____ **AAA Spiral**

Where did you buy it? _____

When? mm/ y y

Why did you choose a AAA Spiral Guide? _____

_____

_____

_____

Did this guide meet your expectations?

Exceeded ☐   Met all ☐   Met most ☐   Fell below ☐

Please give your reasons _____

_____

_____

_____

continued on next page...

Were there any aspects of this guide that you particularly liked?

_____

_____

_____

_____

_____

Is there anything we could have done better?

_____

_____

_____

_____

_____

About you...

Name (Mr/Mrs/Ms) _____

Address _____

_____

_____ **Zip** _____

Daytime tel nos. _____

Which age group are you in?

Under 25 ☐   25–34 ☐   35–44 ☐   45–54 ☐   55–64 ☐   65+ ☐

How many trips do you make a year?

Less than one ☐   One ☐   Two ☐   Three or more ☐

Are you a AAA member? Yes ☐   No ☐

Name of AAA club _____

About your trip...

When did you book? m m / y y   **When did you travel?** m m / y y

How long did you stay? _____

Was it for business or leisure? _____

Did you buy any other travel guides for your trip? ☐ Yes   ☐ No

If yes, which ones? _____

_____

Thank you for taking the time to complete this questionnaire.